Asian
Wraps

Also by Nina Simonds

A Spoonful of Ginger

Asian Noodles

China Express

Classic Chinese Cuisine

China's Food

Chinese Seasons

NINA SIMONDS **Asian**

Wraps

DELICIOUSLY EASY HAND-HELD BUNDLES TO STUFF, WRAP, AND RELISH

PHOTOGRAPHY BY MELANIE ACEVEDO

WILLIAM MORROW AND COMPANY, INC.   NEW YORK

Copyright © 2000 by Nina Simonds
Photographs copyright © 2000 by Melanie Acevedo
Food styling by Rori Spinelli
Prop styling by Christina Wressel

It is the policy of William Morrow and Company, Inc., and its imprints and affiliates,
recognizing the importance of preserving what has been written, to print the books we
publish on acid-free paper, and we exert out best efforts to that end.

Library of Congress Cataloging-in-Publication Data

Simonds, Nina.
Asian wraps: deliciously easy hand-held bundles to stuff, wrap, and relish / Nina Simonds.
p.   cm.
Includes index.
ISBN 0-688-16300-9 (alk. paper)
1. Stuffed foods (Cookery) 2. Cookery, Oriental.   I. Title.
TX836.S55   1999   99-25567
                                         CIP

Printed in the United States of America

First Edition

1 2 3 4 5 6 7 8 9 10

BOOK DESIGN BY LEAH CARLSON-STANISIC

www.williammorrow.com

For my Dad, and in loving memory of my Mom,
who always ordered mu shu and introduced me to the pleasures of Asian wraps

contents

Acknowledgments

Books are often the product of a collaboration between the author and many sources. *Asian Wraps* **is no exception. There are so many people, in this country and in Asia, who have been incredibly generous with their knowledge and time that I'd love to thank them individually, but space won't permit. I must, however, mention a few by name:**

Debby Richards, my dear buddy, and Carol Maynard are superb recipe testers and always ready with invaluable suggestions. Thanks to Julie Lutts for her friendship and fabulous baskets.

Piia Kairento, my ever-faithful Jesse-sitter, and her fiancé, Mario DiMaco, have been incredibly helpful in taking care of my son during my forays to Asia. Special thanks to Karen Cady, who carpools, and then some, while I'm away.

Jane Dystel, my wonderful agent, has shown me how great agents can be.

Mat Schaffer, my pal, who once again came through with great title suggestions, among other things.

At William Morrow, my thanks to Pam Hoenig, my editor, who has been a pleasure to work with, as well as Leah Carlson-Stanisic, Carrie Weinberg, Corinne Alhadeff, Lorie Young, Karen Lumley, and Kate Heddings.

My warmest thanks to Melanie Acevedo for the exquisite photos and her fabulous team, Christina Wressel and Rori Spinelli. And special thanks to potters Teresa Chang and Steven Murphy for the use of their exquisite porcelain dishes and pots in many of the photographs.

I also want to acknowledge the generous support from dear friends, my family, fellow colleagues, editors, and students.

Most of all, I want to thank Don and Jesse Rose, who are a wonderful and constant source of love and joy in my life. I am blessed.

Introduction

As a child, I was weaned on mu shu pork, so I was familiar with the concept of Asian roll-ups early on and I loved them. Who wouldn't? The idea of wrapping food and fillings in wrappers and eating them with your hands is ingenious and fun. But it wasn't until I went to Asia in the early seventies to study Mandarin and Chinese cooking that I realized how vast and diverse the medium was.

The first *real* Asian wraps I tasted were unforgettable. They were called *Amoy Popia,* or fresh Chinese spring rolls, and they were prepared for the "cold food" festival, a holiday celebrated in the spring when only cold foods are eaten, honoring the memory of a dead poet. Delicate, lacy spring roll skins are brushed with pungent hoisin sauce, dusted with crushed peanuts, and filled with garlicky stir-fried vegetables and shrimp. I also sampled minced pigeon and other unusual Cantonese stir-fried dishes that were wrapped in iceberg lettuce. Then I had *dim sum* for the first time, and I couldn't believe all the different types of wraps created by Chinese chefs. I had to try each and every one. There were hundreds of dumplings in all kinds of skins, with meat, seafood, and vegetable fillings.

Soon afterward, a visit to a tiny Vietnamese restaurant took wraps to yet another dimension. I tasted exquisite spring rolls—fresh and fried. The fresh rolls, with their filling of cooked shrimp and fresh herbs, were rolled in softened rice wrappers, and the fried variety was no less delicious, with a vegetable filling and crisp rice paper skin. You wrapped them up in fresh lettuce leaves and dipped them in spicy *nuoc cham,* a fiery sweet-and-sour sauce. I also had grilled beef wrapped in *la lot* leaves (a type of vine indigenous to Southeast Asia) and several types of seasoned barbecued meats wrapped in leafy lettuce. It was all delicious.

This book brings together a collection of some of my favorite Asian wraps or roll-up dishes, as well as some new recipes that I created for the book. It's a fertile field. While the idea of wrapping food in

1

different skins and eating it with your fingers is quite traditional and primal, the concept is especially appropriate for today's lifestyle. Since wraps are fresh, healthy, and easy to prepare, they are ideal for the contemporary cook. They can be served as appetizers to pique the palate or as sumptuous meal-in-one dishes.

While many of these recipes are renditions of traditional dishes, feel free to improvise and use what's available. Like any finger food, wraps are meant to be casual and seasonal, so they can be adapted to suit the time and place. Personally, I can't think of a more appealing way to eat.

NINA SIMONDS
Spring 1999

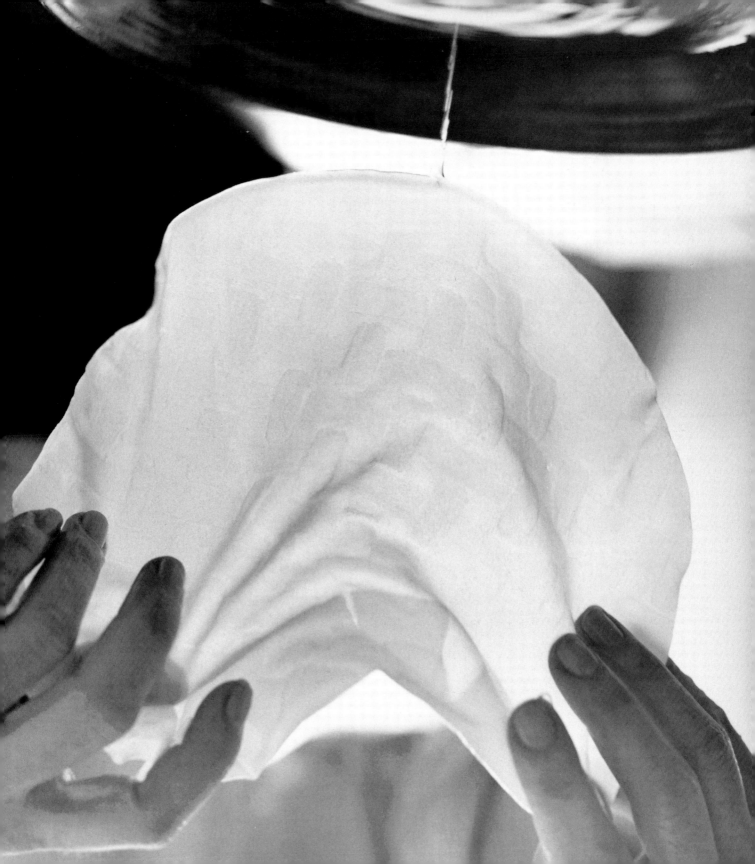

ASIAN WRAP BASICS

Asian wraps or roll-ups are a varied lot, depending on their filling and composition, but they all share the unique trait of being rolled up in a wrapper. And the wrappers are extraordinarily diverse.

These days, except for rare occasions or for special guests, I rarely prepare handmade wrappers, preferring instead to purchase them in ethnic stores or supermarkets. Although dumpling and spring roll wrappers are available in many supermarkets, I generally prefer to buy wrappers in Asian markets, since they are usually of a better quality. Check the refrigerators first for fresh wrappers. Both Asian specialty stores and supermarkets often have a local supplier who provides fresh products. Choose the thinnest wrappers, since they will make the most refined roll-ups.

If fresh wrappers aren't available, most Asian markets carry a supply of frozen varieties. Make certain to check for freezer burn and let the wrappers defrost completely before using them.

This chapter will introduce you to the diverse family of Asian wrappers. The glossary gives basic information, while the chart shows the wrappers' primary uses, with suggestions for substitutes. If a particular wrapper is unavailable, don't hesitate to use the next best ingredient on hand.

The Wrappers

In Asia, the wrapper may take the form of a wheat or rice flour skin (such as a spring roll skin, Mandarin pancake, or dumpling skin), some type of leafy green, a square of seaweed, or a steamed or baked bread. For those admirable souls who have the time and inclination, I've included recipes for basic wrappers. The following glossary gives the information you'll need for all the wrappers used in this book.

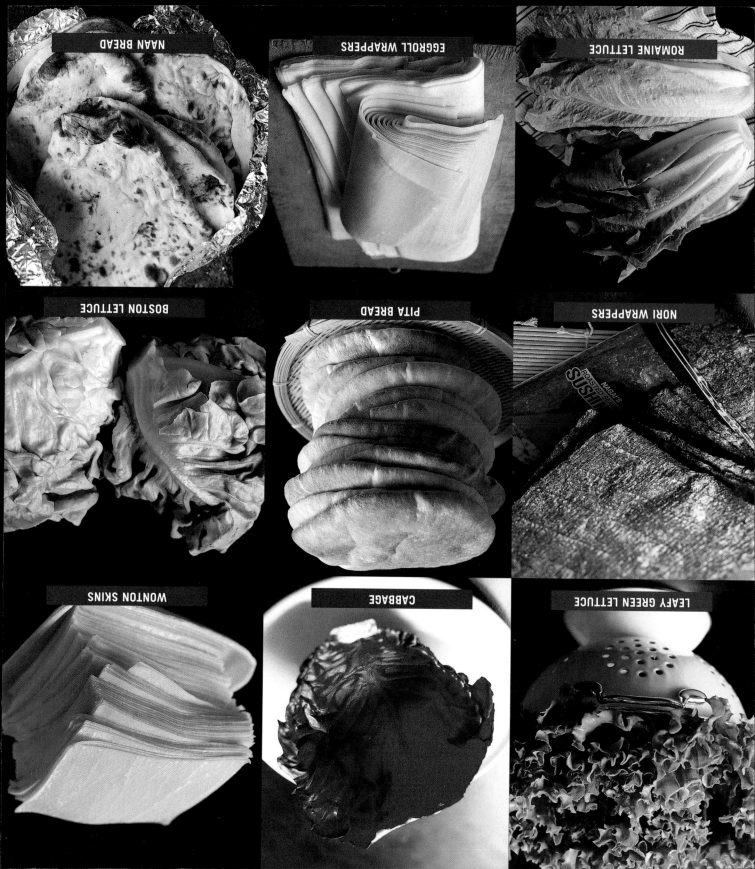

NAAN BREAD

EGGROLL WRAPPERS

ROMAINE LETTUCE

BOSTON LETTUCE

PITA BREAD

NORI WRAPPERS

WONTON SKINS

CABBAGE

LEAFY GREEN LETTUCE

LAVASH BREAD

FLOUR TORTILLAS

LOTUS LEAVES

SPRING ROLL WRAPPERS

NAPA CABBAGE

DUMPLING WRAPPERS

RADICCHIO

RICE WRAPPERS

DUMPLING SKINS: Also labeled wonton skins, *shao mai*, or *gyoza* skins, dumpling skins are widely available in supermarket produce sections and Asian markets. Thin fresh skins are preferred, particularly for steamed dumplings. Generally, round wheat-flour wrappers are used for boiled and steamed dumplings; square skins, made with an egg dough, are usually boiled and deep-fried for wontons. Fresh skins will keep for up to a week in the refrigerator and they can be frozen and defrosted for later use.

MANDARIN PANCAKES: A staple in northern China, Mandarin pancakes are mainly known for accompanying such notable dishes as Peking and camphor-smoked duck and mu shu pork. In fact, they can be served with any stir-fried mixture and used as wrappers. You can make your own (see page 12), order them as take-out from a Chinese restaurant, or buy them frozen in an Asian market.

LEAFY GREENS: While uncooked vegetables were not traditionally eaten in Asia, today numerous greens are popular in salads, on cold platters, and as wrappers, especially in Vietnamese, Thai, Malaysian, and Chinese dishes. Spinach, watercress, and leafy and iceberg lettuces are the most common varieties there, but in the West we are blessed with a wealth of greens. The varieties most widely used as wrappers are:

CHINESE CABBAGE: Although the Chinese grow numerous varieties of cabbage, Napa, with its broad, oval leaves, and Peking, which is rather thin but leafy, are the most useful for roll-up dishes. Choose cabbages with broad, leafy leaves and beware of spots or rotten cores. Usually I suggest blanching the leaves for a minute in boiling water and refreshing them immediately under cold running water to soften the leaves and keep the color vibrant.

CONVENTIONAL CABBAGE: For wraps, I recommend using green or red cabbage, with wide, round leaves, or Savoy cabbage, with crinkly leaves. As for Chinese cabbage, I suggest blanching the leaves briefly in boiling water and refreshing them under cold running water.

LETTUCES:
Boston: This is probably my favorite lettuce wrapper because of its ample size, round shape, and crisp yet tender texture. Like any other lettuce, it should be rinsed, the core trimmed, and the leaves drained on paper towels. I prepare the lettuce several hours ahead, wrap it in paper towels, and store it in plastic bags in the refrigerator.

Bibb: Considered by many to be the most refined of the buttery lettuces, Bibb has a texture similar to that of Boston lettuce, but some say it holds up better to dressings. The leaves tend to be smaller than those of Boston lettuce.

Iceberg: Many Americans have gone beyond iceberg, preferring the more colorful and flavorful specialty lettuces, but iceberg is often ideal as a fresh wrapper for Asian roll-up dishes. Its crisp texture makes it very appealing.

Leafy (red and green): Both the red and green varieties of leafy or loose-leaf lettuces are extremely popular as fresh wrappers for myriad roll-up dishes. Their pliable yet crisp texture lends itself nicely to roll-ups, though they often wilt more quickly than romaine, Boston, and Bibb.

Romaine: You might say romaine is the new star of the American green-market, since its popularity now outshines that of iceberg. Romaine has a pleasing assertive and less buttery flavor than Bibb and Boston lettuce. I like to use it as a wrapper for spicy dishes that require a stronger flavor.

Radicchio: While radicchio, a slightly bitter "green" with reddish purple leaves wrapped in a small, tight head, is not traditionally used as an Asian wrapper, its flavor complements a number of grilled dishes beautifully.

INDIAN FLATBREAD: Indian cooks make wonderful flatbreads that are cooked and baked in skillets and tandoor ovens. They are made with wheat, corn, and lentils and most are superb as wrappers. For this book, I adapted a leavened flatbread (*naan*) that is easy to prepare and complements many of the vegetarian dishes (and others) beautifully.

LAVASH: Near Eastern cooks bake large, paper-thin flatbreads known as lavash from wheat flour, yeast, salt, and water. These have become very popular and are now sold in well-stocked supermarkets and health food stores; a superior fresh product can be found in ethnic markets and bakeries. Lavash keeps well in the refrigerator and freezer.

LOTUS LEAVES: Chinese cooks love to steam sweet rice mixed with bits of chicken, pork, black mushrooms, and other savory ingredients in lotus leaves for the unusual perfume the leaves lend to the food. The leaves are not eaten. Dried lotus leaves, which are sold at most Asian markets, should not be confused with dried thin bamboo leaves. The leaves should be softened in hot water before use.

NORI OR SEAWEED WRAPPERS: Nori, or purple laver, is seaweed that has been cleaned and dried in sheets.

Westerners know it as the wrapper for sushi, but it is also used as a garnish for numerous dishes, cut into strips or crumbled. The quality varies; usually the price will be a good clue. The costlier brands are often sold in boxes and tins. Most sushi experts suggest lightly toasting nori to bring out its flavor. To toast nori, hold the sheet with tongs, for 5 seconds on one side, over an open flame.

PITA BREAD: Not long ago, pita bread, a leavened wheat-flour flatbread, was only available in Near Eastern markets, but now, thanks to its general appeal, it is sold in any well-stocked supermarket. If possible, buy pita baked by local ethnic producers. Pita bread freezes well and will keep in the refrigerator for up to ten days.

RICE PAPER WRAPPERS: *Banh trang*, or rice paper wrappers, are round or triangular translucent sheets made from rice flour, salt, and water. (The unique pattern on the sheets is created when they are dried on bamboo trays.) Although they are brittle when dried, once dipped in hot water, they become soft and pliable in seconds. Traditionally, the rounds are used for roll-ups and the triangular pieces to wrap grilled meats and as

wrappers for deep-fried finger foods. Once opened, the package should be stored in an airtight plastic bag.

SPRING ROLL SKINS (LUMPIA WRAPPERS): While Western cooks are most familiar with egg roll wrappers made with a pasta-like egg dough, Chinese cooks prefer lacy skins made by rubbing a wheat-flour-and-water dough over a hot griddle. They are more delicate for wrapping stir-fried foods and, once deep-fried, they tend to stay crisp. Lumpia wrappers are commonly sold frozen in Asian markets. Defrost them and separate them by hand, then cover with a damp towel as you work, since they tend to dry out quickly.

WHEAT-FLOUR TORTILLAS: Much as the Chinese relish plain, unleavened griddle-baked pancakes to wrap up many of their dishes, so too do Mexicans. Of course, Mexican cooks make their pancakes, or tortillas, with flour or corn. Many supermarkets carry a good-quality flour tortilla that, lightly brushed with toasted sesame oil and steamed, makes a good wrapper for Asian dishes.

USING THE WRAPPERS

Asian wrappers are a varied lot and often easily interchangeable. The following chart gives the main uses for a number of wrappers with suggested substitutions.

WRAPPER	USE	SPECIAL TIPS	SUBSTITUTIONS
Dumpling skins	Panfried, deep-fried, steamed, and boiled dumplings	Choose thin skins	Wonton skins
Mandarin pancakes	Stir-fries, barbecued poultry and meats	Look for thin pancakes	Good-quality flour tortillas
Leafy greens	Salads and stir-fries		Spinach or watercress, flour tortillas
Chinese cabbage	Stir-fries and stews		White cabbage
Indian flatbreads	Stir-fries and stews		Lavash, pita bread
Lavash	Stir-fries and stews		Thin pita bread
Lotus leaves	Steamed packages		Parchment paper
Nori (seaweed)	Sushi and salads	Toast to bring out flavor	
Pita bread	Stir-fries and stews		Lavash, Indian flatbreads
Rice paper wrappers	Fresh and fried rolls		Spring roll skins
Spring roll skins	Fresh and fried rolls		Flour tortillas

Mandarin Pancakes

The secret to great Mandarin pancakes is rolling the dough thin and twirling the pancakes in a hot pan to cook them evenly on both sides so they puff up and the inside steams. Only then should the two pancakes be separated.

2 cups all-purpose flour
1 cup boiling water
¼ cup toasted sesame oil

1. Place the flour in a medium-size bowl and stir in the boiling water with a wooden spoon until a rough dough forms. Let cool slightly, then turn the dough out onto a lightly floured work surface. Knead for several minutes, until smooth and elastic, sprinkling in some flour if the dough is wet.

2. Cut the dough in half. Cover one half with a kitchen towel and roll out the other half into a long snake-like roll about 1¼ inches thick. Cut the roll into 8 pieces and cover the pieces with a towel. Repeat with the remaining dough.

3. Place one piece of the dough, cut side down, on a lightly floured work surface and press to flatten to a 2-inch circle. Set aside. (Alternatively, you can flatten the dough in a tortilla press.) Flatten another piece of dough and brush the top with the toasted sesame oil. Place the first piece of flattened dough on top and press the two pieces together. Using a small slender rolling pin, roll out to a 4-inch circle. Set aside on a lightly floured tray and cover with a dish towel while you prepare the remaining pancakes, adding the finished pancakes to the tray.

4. Heat a well-seasoned crêpe pan or a nonstick griddle until very hot. (A drop of water sprinkled on the surface should evaporate immediately.) Place one double pancake in the hot pan and fry, twirling the pancake in a circular motion with your fingertips so that it doesn't stick, until it puffs in the middle, about a minute. Flip over and cook, again twirling the pancake with your fingertips, for about 1 minute longer. Remove from the heat and drop the pancake onto the work surface. Let cool slightly, then peel the two pancakes apart. Fold each one into quarters, with the cooked surface inside. Repeat the process with the remaining pancakes, arranging them overlapping in a circle on a steamer tray or heatproof serving plate. Cover until you are ready to serve.

5. Before serving, steam the pancakes for about 5 minutes over boiling water. Use as directed in the recipe.

MAKES 16 PANCAKES

Basic Chinese Yeast Dough

Chinese doughs have the same ingredients as Western bread doughs: flour, yeast, and water. The two main differences are that this dough rises for double or triple the usual rising time and baking powder is added just before the bread is steamed. This insures a light, airy bread. Once the dough has risen, you can make many different shapes, such as silver-thread loaves and flower buns.

1. With a wooden spoon, mix together the sugar and water in a large bowl, stirring to dissolve the sugar. Add the yeast and stir again to dissolve it.

2. Add the flour and 1 tablespoon of the oil, stirring with the wooden spoon to form a rough dough. Turn the dough out onto a lightly floured work surface, scraping it from the sides of the bowl. Knead lightly until the dough is smooth and elastic, about 10 minutes, adding a little more flour if the dough is too sticky. (The consistency may vary slightly depending on the weather: If the dough is too dry, add a little warm water.)

3. Brush the large bowl with the remaining ½ tablespoon oil and put the dough in the bowl. Turn to coat. Cover with a damp dish towel and place in a warm, draft-free place (like a turned-off oven with a pilot light). Let rise until tripled in bulk, about 3 hours. Use as directed in the recipe.

2½ tablespoons sugar
1 cup warm water
1½ teaspoons active dry yeast (about half a packet)
3 cups all-purpose flour, or more as needed
1½ tablespoons corn oil

MAKES 18 BUNS

Steamed Lotus Buns

Lotus buns are one of the easiest and most attractive shapes to make with the Basic Chinese Yeast Dough. I love to stuff these rolls with myriad meat, seafood, or vegetable mixtures to make a type of Chinese sandwich. They reheat beautifully if steamed for several minutes.

1 recipe Basic Chinese Yeast Dough
    (page 13)
1¼ teaspoons baking powder
¼ cup toasted sesame oil

1. Turn the risen dough out onto a lightly floured work surface. Flatten it into a circle with your hands and put the baking powder in the center. Gather up the edges to enclose the baking powder, bring them together, and pinch together in the center. Knead the dough lightly to incorporate the baking powder evenly.

2. Roll the dough out on the lightly floured surface into a long snake-like roll about 1½ inches in diameter. Cut the roll into 18 pieces.

3. Place each piece, cut side down, on the work surface and, using a small slender rolling pin, roll each piece out into a 3-inch circle. Brush the surface generously with the sesame oil and fold over to form a half-moon shape. With a sharp knife, lightly score the surface of the bun with a diamond pattern. Make two equally spaced V-shaped indentations in the round edge of the bun with the blunt edge of a knife. Place the bun on a cookie sheet lined with wax or parchment paper and repeat with the remaining dough. Cover with a damp dish towel and let rise for 20 minutes.

4. Fill a wok or a large pot with several inches of water and bring to a boil. Arrange the risen buns on a steaming tray or an aluminum pie plate punched with holes and very lightly brushed with corn or toasted sesame oil. To hold the steaming tray steady above the boiling water, crisscross chopsticks in the wok or set an empty tuna can with both ends removed in the center of it. Place the tray or plate of buns over the boiling water. Cover and steam until the buns are light and springy, about 15 minutes. Remove with a spatula and serve hot or at room temperature.

5. To reheat, the buns steam for several minutes or microwave, covered with a damp dish towel, just until hot. To serve, stuff the buns with the meat, seafood, or vegetable mixture as directed in the recipes.

MAKES 18 BUNS

Indian Flatbread

According to Indian food authority Madhur Jaffrey, this leavened flatbread, known as *naan,* is traditionally shaped like a teardrop and slapped onto the wall of a tandoor oven, where it bakes. Madhur has developed a clever method of broiling the dough. I like to do something in between, by baking the dough in a very, very hot conventional oven. I also like to sprinkle minced scallion greens on top for extra flavor.

3¾ cups all-purpose flour
1 teaspoon salt
1½ teaspoons active dry yeast (about half a packet)
¾ cup warm milk
¾ cup plain yogurt
1 teaspoon baking powder
3 tablespoons safflower or corn oil
½ cup minced scallion greens

1. Mix the flour and salt together in a large bowl. Add the yeast to the milk in a small bowl, stirring to dissolve, then add it to the flour along with the yogurt and baking powder, mixing with a wooden spoon until you have a rough dough. (Add a little warm water if the dough seems dry.)

2. Turn the dough out onto a lightly floured work surface and knead until smooth and elastic, about 10 minutes. Return it to the bowl, cover with a damp dish towel, and put it in a warm, draft-free place (like a turned-off oven with a pilot light). Let rise for about 1½ hours.

3. Remove the dough from the oven if you've put it there. Preheat the oven to 450 degrees F.

4. Turn the dough out again onto a lightly floured surface and shape into a long roll about 2 inches in diameter. Cut into 18 pieces. Cover with a damp dish towel to keep it from drying out as you work. One at a time, roll each piece of dough with a small slender rolling pin into a 6-inch circle. Arrange on cookie sheets that have been lightly brushed with the oil. Brush the center of each circle with water and sprinkle with the minced scallions.

5. Bake the breads for 3 minutes, flip over, and bake until both sides are golden brown, about 2 more minutes. Remove, let cool slightly, and serve.

MAKES 18 FLATBREADS

Basic Chinese Chicken Broth

1. Combine the water with the chicken bones, rice wine, and ginger slices in a large pot and bring to a boil. Reduce the heat to low and simmer, uncovered, for 1½ hours, skimming the surface to remove any impurities.

2. Strain the broth through a fine-meshed strainer, removing the bones or chicken pieces, and skim to remove any fat.

3. Use as directed in the individual recipes.

MAKES ABOUT 6 CUPS

9 cups water
2½ pounds chicken backs, necks, bones, and/or pieces
1 cup rice wine or sake
6 slices fresh ginger, about the size of a quarter, lightly smashed with the flat edge of a knife

USING THE RECIPES

🌀 Read the recipes thoroughly before preparing the dishes.

🌀 Before you start cooking, set up trays with the marinated and cut meats, seafood, and vegetables, the prepared seasonings, and the premixed sauces neatly organized by your stove. Particularly with stir-fried dishes, having everything lined up in advance makes last-minute execution of the dish easy.

🌀 Generally, recipes are for six servings. To prepare two or three servings, divide the recipe in half.

🌀 Use fresh, seasonal, top-quality ingredients. Don't be afraid to substitute foods that are available in your market, as appropriate, or improvise with new foods.

🌀 Usually, the water chestnuts called for are canned. They should be blanched in boiling water for 10 seconds, then refreshed under cold running water and drained. When using fresh water chestnuts, first peel them, then cook them for 5 minutes in boiling water to remove the starchy quality.

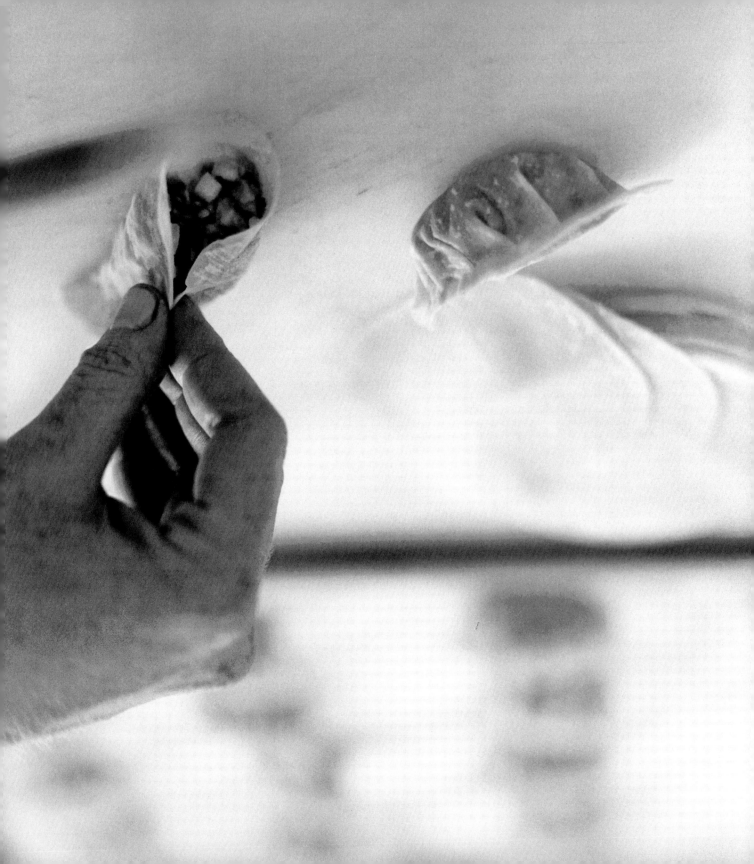

Bite-size
Wraps | APPETIZERS AND STARTERS

BARBECUED SWEET-AND-SOUR SHRIMP ❧ VEGETARIAN WONTONS ❧ PORK SATÉ WITH RADICCHIO ❧ SPICY SICHUAN-STYLE WONTONS ❧ CHINESE MEAT DUMPLINGS ❧ STEAMED OPEN-TOPPED DUMPLINGS ❧ FLAKY CURRY TURNOVERS ❧ VEGETABLE SAMOSAS ❧ VIETNAMESE SPRING ROLLS ❧ FRESH CHINESE SPRING ROLLS ❧ CANTONESE SPRING ROLLS ❧ CRISP VIETNAMESE SHRIMP FINGERS WITH FRESH HERBS ❧ LOTUS CHICKEN PACKAGES ❧ BASIC SUSHI ❧ HAND-ROLLED SUSHI WITH SMOKED SALMON ❧

Asia boasts a wonderful variety of roll-ups and wraps that are often served as starters or hors d'oeuvres. Their compact shapes and enticing textures beguile the palate and pique the appetite, teasing it with bursts of pungent flavors.

In Vietnam, fresh and fried spring rolls stuffed with fillings of plump shrimp, barbecued pork, shredded vegetables, delicate rice noodles, and fresh herbs are served with a sumptuous peanut sauce or a heady sweet-and-sour dipping sauce. The opaque dried skins, which are made of rice flour and water, magically transform themselves into translucent, pliable wrappers once dipped in hot water. The flavors of Vietnamese spring rolls are clean and inviting, the perfect opening for any meal. (I often serve them on their own as a light lunch or dinner.)

Chinese roll-ups are even more diverse, mainly because of the different skins: Small round wheat-flour-and-water or rice flour wrappers, folded in the shape of dumplings, envelop sumptuous, savory stuffings made with meat, seafood, or vegetables. These dumplings may be pleated, straight-edged, or open-topped and boiled, deep-fried, or steamed. Small square wheat-flour wrappers are also filled with meat, seafood, or vegetables, then folded and shaped to form wontons, which may be boiled or deep-fried. Northern-style Chinese dumplings, which are plump with cabbage, pork or lamb, and garlic chives, are hearty and robust, whereas the southern and eastern Chinese dumplings, which are studded with more costly ingredients such as shrimp, black mushrooms, shark's fin, and crab roe, are delicate and refined. All are delicious.

In Japan, the most distinguished and coveted of roll-ups is sushi, which invariably includes seasoned cooked rice. The fillings, topping, and wrappers may vary, but the sticky, faintly sweet-and-sour rice is the constant. The most familiar forms to Westerners are those wrapped in seaweed (*nori*) or covered with fresh seafood (*sashimi*), but there are numerous others, depending on the ingredients at hand, the shape, and the region. I like to create different types of sushi: For one, I shape rolls of rice by hand, encircling them with thin slices of smoked salmon and seasoning them with capers and slivers of red onion.

Many Asian roll-ups, such as satés (grilled meats or seafood served with a coconut-peanut sauce), are wrapped in lettuce leaves, a fresh counterpoint to the cooked food within. Different pungent marinades and dipping sauces broaden the repertoire. Other wraps, like turnovers and samosas, are cooked in flaky pastry and their fillings may be meaty or vegetarian.

I often improvise roll-up dishes by stir-frying different meats and vegetables in a variety of sauces, then serving the hot food wrapped in lettuce leaves or steamed flour tortillas. My guests always love them and they're perfect for entertaining. They're casual and appealing, because you can eat them with your fingers and guests can help themselves. Best of all, many of the recipes can be prepared completely in advance and cooked or reheated at the last minute so the host can relax and have a good time as well.

Barbecued Sweet-and-Sour Shrimp

In this irresistible dish, succulently tender shrimp are glazed with a vibrant sweet-and-sour sauce and grilled with pineapple and scallions, then served with a wrapping of fresh lettuce. Other types of seafood or chicken would be equally delicious.

1¾ pounds medium-size raw shrimp, peeled, deveined, rinsed, drained, and patted dry

FOR THE MARINADE, mixed together:

¼ cup rice wine or sake

2 tablespoons peeled and minced fresh ginger

1 tablespoon minced garlic

1 tablespoon toasted sesame oil

FOR THE SWEET-AND-SOUR SAUCE:

1 cup ketchup

½ cup plus 2 tablespoons sugar

½ cup water

6 tablespoons Japanese rice vinegar

2 teaspoons soy sauce

1 teaspoon salt

1½ teaspoons cornstarch

FOR THE GRILL:

1 ripe pineapple (about 2 pounds), peeled, cored, and cut into cubes, or about 2½ cups drained canned pineapple chunks

6 scallions, ends trimmed and cut into 1-inch sections

Twelve 10-inch-long bamboo skewers, soaked in cold water for 1 hour and drained

2 tablespoons safflower or corn oil

TO SERVE:

2 heads Boston lettuce, cores trimmed, leaves separated, pressed to flatten, rinsed, drained, and arranged in a serving bowl or basket

1. Place the shrimp in a large bowl and add the marinade. Toss lightly to coat, and cover with plastic wrap. Refrigerate for 20 minutes.

2. Combine the sweet-and-sour sauce ingredients in a medium-size heavy saucepan, stirring to dissolve the sugar. Heat, stirring, until thickened. Pour half the sweet-and-sour sauce into a bowl and set aside. Keep the remaining sauce warm over low heat.

3. Alternately thread the shrimp, pineapple cubes, and scallions onto the bamboo skewers and brush with the reserved sweet-and-sour sauce.

4. Prepare a medium-hot fire for grilling. Place the grill rack about 3 inches above the coals. Brush the grill rack generously with the safflower or corn oil and heat until hot. Arrange the skewers of shrimp on the grill and grill until the shrimp are cooked through, 3 to 4 minutes per side.

5. Remove and arrange on a serving platter. Pour the remaining hot sweet-and-sour sauce into a serving dish. To eat, spread a dollop of the sweet-and-sour sauce on a lettuce leaf, arrange some of the grilled shrimp, pineapple, and scallions on top, roll up, tucking in the edges, and eat with your fingers.

MAKES 6 SERVINGS

Vegetarian Wontons

Wontons are always a popular appetizer, and these are no exception. Even meat eaters are impressed, since they are bursting with vibrant seasonings. I like to make a bunch, fry them in batches, drain, cool, and freeze them in plastic bags, then defrost and reheat them in a medium-hot oven as needed.

1 pound firm tofu, cut horizontally through the thickness into ½-inch-thick slices

14 dried Chinese black mushrooms, softened in hot water to cover, drained, and stems removed

¾ cup canned whole water chestnuts, blanched in boiling water for 10 seconds, refreshed under cold running water, drained, blotted dry, and chopped

1½ cups grated carrots

FOR THE SEASONINGS:

2 tablespoons peeled and minced fresh ginger

1½ tablespoons minced scallion whites

1 tablespoon soy sauce

1½ teaspoons salt, or to taste

1¼ teaspoons toasted sesame oil

TO FINISH THE FILLING:

1 large egg, lightly beaten

1 large egg white, lightly beaten

3 to 4 tablespoons cornstarch, as needed

TO MAKE AND FRY THE WONTONS:

50 wonton skins

Cornstarch as needed

4 cups safflower or corn oil

TO SERVE:

Chinese plum or duck sauce

Chinese hot mustard

1. Wrap the tofu slices in paper towels or a cotton dish towel, place on a plate, and put a heavy weight, such as a cast-iron skillet, on top. Let stand for 30 minutes to press out the excess water.

2. Transfer the tofu to a large bowl and, using a fork, mash until smooth.

3. Shred the black mushroom caps by hand or mince in a food processor fitted with the steel blade. Add the mushrooms, water chestnuts, 1 cup of the carrots, and the seasonings to the bowl with the tofu and stir vigorously to mix well. Add the egg, egg white, and 3 tablespoons of the cornstarch and mix until smooth and sticky. Add the remaining cornstarch if the mixture doesn't hold together well.

4. Place a teaspoon of the filling in the center of each wonton skin, fold it over diagonally to form a triangle, and press the edges together to enclose the filling. Dab a little water on the opposite corners of the wonton skin and press together to form a tortellini-like shape. Place the finished wontons on a cookie sheet that has been lightly dusted with cornstarch.

5. Heat a wok or a deep heavy skillet over high heat, add the oil, and heat to 375 degrees F. Fry the wontons in batches without crowding them, turning constantly, until a deep golden brown. Remove with a handled strainer, drain briefly, and place on paper towels to remove the excess oil. Arrange the fried wontons on a serving platter and serve with plum sauce or duck sauce and hot mustard.

MAKES 50 WONTONS

Pork Saté with Radicchio

Radicchio has a slightly bitter flavor, but the crisp freshness of this green contrasts beautifully with the coconut-peanut saté sauce. In addition to pork, saté can be made with chicken, beef, or seafood.

1¼ pounds pork tenderloin, trimmed of any fat or gristle

FOR THE MARINADE, mixed together:
⅓ cup fish sauce
¼ cup minced fresh lemongrass (ends trimmed and outer leaves removed)
3½ tablespoons minced garlic

TO GRILL:
2 tablespoons safflower or corn oil
Twelve to fourteen 10-inch-long bamboo skewers, soaked in cold water for 1 hour and drained

TO SERVE:
2 to 3 heads radicchio, cores trimmed, leaves separated, pressed to flatten, rinsed, and drained
3 medium-size carrots, finely shredded or grated (about 1½ cups)
3 tablespoons chopped cilantro (fresh coriander) leaves
Saté Sauce (page 148)

1. Cut the pork tenderloin into ⅛-inch-thick slices. Place in a medium-size bowl, add the marinade, and toss lightly to coat. Cover with plastic wrap and let sit for at least 2 hours in the refrigerator.

2. Prepare a medium-hot fire for grilling or preheat the broiler. Place the grill rack 3 inches above the coals. Brush the grill rack with the oil. (Alternatively, you can heat a large heavy skillet, add a teaspoon of oil, and heat until near smoking over high heat.)

3. Thread several pork slices onto each bamboo skewer.

4. Arrange the radicchio leaves in overlapping rows on a serving platter and sprinkle little bunches of the shredded carrots on top.

5. Grill or broil the pork slices (or panfry in the skillet) until cooked all the way through, about 6 minutes per side. Remove and let cool slightly.

6. Arrange several pieces of meat over the shredded carrots on each radicchio leaf. Sprinkle with the chopped cilantro. To eat, spoon some of the saté sauce on top of each portion and eat with your fingers.

MAKES 6 SERVINGS

Spicy Sichuan-Style Wontons

While I've sampled this dim sum in a number of restaurants, my favorite version is prepared by master chef C. K. Sau at the New Shanghai in Boston; his sesame sauce is especially delicious. The versatile sauce is also wonderful with noodles. I make it in large batches, since it will keep in the refrigerator for weeks.

1 pound lean ground pork
¾ cup canned whole water chestnuts, blanched in boiling water for 10 seconds, refreshed under cold running water, drained, blotted dry, and chopped

FOR THE SEASONINGS, mixed together:
2½ tablespoons peeled and minced fresh ginger
2½ tablespoons minced scallion whites
2½ tablespoons soy sauce
1½ tablespoons rice wine or sake
2½ teaspoons toasted sesame oil
1½ tablespoons cornstarch

FOR THE WONTONS:
50 wonton skins
Cornstarch as needed

TO COOK THE WONTONS:
3 quarts water

FOR THE SPICY SESAME SAUCE, processed until smooth in a food processor or blender:
8 cloves garlic, peeled
Two 1-inch square knobs fresh ginger, peeled
1 teaspoon crushed red pepper
6 tablespoons Chinese toasted sesame paste (mix well before adding)

¼ cup toasted sesame oil
5 tablespoons soy sauce
¼ cup rice wine or sake
1½ tablespoons Chinese black vinegar or Worcestershire sauce
1½ tablespoons sugar
6 tablespoons chicken broth or water

1. In a medium-size bowl, combine the ground pork, water chestnuts, and seasonings and stir vigorously.

2. Place a teaspoon of the filling in the center of each wonton skin, bring the edges up over the filling, and press together to enclose the filling and form a money-bag-like shape. Place the finished wontons on a cookie sheet that has been lightly dusted with cornstarch.

3. In a deep pot, heat the water until boiling. Add the wontons and cook for about 8 minutes, until the filling is cooked, reducing the heat to medium when the water reaches a boil again. Remove the wontons with a handled strainer, or drain in a colander, and arrange on a serving platter or in a serving dish with a lip. Drizzle the spicy sesame sauce on top and serve.

MAKES 50 WONTONS

Chinese Meat Dumplings

Chinese meat dumplings make me feel nostalgic for my student days in Taiwan, when we would visit our favorite dumpling shop and fill ourselves with crusty brown pot-stickers and luscious steamed dumplings plump with juice. My favorites are the most traditional: They're stuffed with cabbage, pork, and garlic chives and boiled. I double the recipe and freeze half of them uncooked. Later I throw them into boiling water for an easy, instant, satisfying meal. Dumpling wrappers are often labeled "gyoza" skins in Asian markets.

5 cups cored and finely minced
    Chinese (Napa) cabbage
1 teaspoon salt
1 pound lean ground pork
2 cups finely minced fresh Chinese
    garlic chives (if unavailable,
    substitute 1 cup minced leeks—
    mostly the whites—plus
    1 tablespoon minced garlic)

FOR THE SEASONINGS, mixed together:
2½ tablespoons soy sauce
2 tablespoons toasted sesame oil
1½ tablespoons rice wine
1½ tablespoons peeled and minced
    fresh ginger
1 tablespoon cornstarch, or more as
    needed

**TO FORM, COOK, AND SERVE THE
DUMPLINGS:**
50 dumpling or gyoza skins
Cornstarch as needed
3 quarts water
Dipping sauces (pages 149–152)

1. In a large bowl, combine the cabbage and salt and let sit for 30 minutes. (This will draw water out of the cabbage.)

2. Squeeze as much water as possible out of the cabbage and combine the cabbage with the ground pork, minced chives, and seasonings in a large bowl. Stir vigorously. If the mixture seems loose, add another teaspoon of cornstarch.

3. Place a teaspoon of filling in the center of each dumpling skin and fold the skin over to make a half-moon shape. Spread a little water along the edge of the skin and use the thumb and index finger of one hand to form small pleats along the outside edge of the skin; the inside edge of the dumpling should curve in a semicircular fashion to conform to the shape of the pleated edge. Place the sealed dumplings on a baking sheet lightly dusted with cornstarch.

4. In a large pot, heat the water until boiling. Add half the dumplings, stirring to prevent them from sticking together, and, once the water boils again, cook for 5 minutes. Remove with a handled strainer and drain, then cook the remaining dumplings. Serve the dumplings with the dipping sauces.

MAKES 50 DUMPLINGS

Steamed Open-Topped Dumplings

Dumplings are a diverse medium, with myriad skins and fillings. They can be rustic and crusty, like pot-stickers from northern China, or refined and somewhat elegant, as are these steamed dumplings from eastern China. Serve them with a fragrant black-vinegar-and-soy sauce garnished with shreds of fresh ginger.

1. In a medium-size bowl, combine the ground pork, shrimp, water chestnuts, and seasonings and stir together vigorously. The mixture should be stiff.

2. Line two steamer trays with parchment paper, or use two aluminum pie plates punched with holes and lightly brushed with sesame oil.

3. Place a heaping tablespoon of the filling in the center of each dumpling skin and gather up the edges of the skin around the filling. Holding the dumpling between your index finger and thumb, push the filling up from the bottom and squeeze the dumpling in the middle to create a "waist." Smooth the top of the filling. Place the dumplings ¼ inch apart on the steamer trays.

4. Fill a wok with water level with the bottom edge of the steamer tray, or just below if using pie pans, and heat until boiling. Stack the two steamer trays if possible, cover, and steam over high heat until cooked through, about 15 minutes, reversing the position of the steamers halfway through the cooking time.

5. Sprinkle the tops of the cooked dumplings with the scallion greens. Serve with the dipping sauce. (To reheat the dumplings, steam until piping hot, 5 to 7 minutes.)

MAKES 44 DUMPLINGS

⅔ pound ground lean boneless pork butt

1 pound medium-size shrimp, peeled, deveined, rinsed, drained, blotted dry, and cut into small dice

¾ cup canned whole water chestnuts, blanched in boiling water for 10 seconds, refreshed under cold running water, drained, blotted dry, and coarsely chopped

FOR THE SEASONINGS, mixed together:

2½ tablespoons minced scallion whites

2½ tablespoons peeled and minced fresh ginger

2½ tablespoons soy sauce

2 tablespoons rice wine or sake

2 teaspoons toasted sesame oil

1 large egg white, lightly beaten

2 tablespoons cornstarch

TO FORM AND SERVE THE DUMPLINGS:

Toasted sesame oil as needed

44 dumplings or gyoza skins

3 tablespoons minced scallion greens

Soy Dipping Sauce, Variation I (page 149)

Flaky Curry Turnovers

These flaky curry turnovers are one of my favorite appetizers. I first sampled them in Taipei at a Cantonese dim sum parlor. I've adapted the recipe to suit my own tastes, substituting butter for lard in the pastry and ground turkey for the pork in the filling.

FOR THE TURNOVER PASTRY:
2 cups all-purpose flour
1 teaspoon salt
⅔ cup (10⅔ tablespoons) chilled unsalted butter, cut into tablespoon-size pieces
1 large egg, lightly beaten
4 to 5 tablespoons cold water, as needed

FOR THE FILLING:
½ pound lean ground turkey or beef
2 teaspoons soy sauce
1 tablespoon peeled and minced fresh ginger
1 teaspoon toasted sesame oil
2 tablespoons corn or canola oil
2 medium-size red onions, finely diced (about 2 cups)
1 tablespoon curry powder, preferably Madras curry
1 cup cooked fresh or thawed frozen peas

FOR THE SAUCE, mixed together:
½ cup Basic Chinese Chicken Broth (page 17)
1½ teaspoons sugar
1 teaspoon salt
1 tablespoon cornstarch

TO FINISH THE TURNOVERS:
1 large egg, lightly beaten with 2 tablespoons water

1. Combine the flour and salt in a food processor fitted with the steel blade and pulse to blend. Add the butter and pulse until the mixture resembles cornmeal. Combine the egg and ¼ cup of the cold water. With the machine running, slowly add the egg mixture and process just until roughly combined. Add up to a tablespoon more water if the mixture is dry. Turn out onto a lightly floured surface and, using the heels of your hands, lightly knead the mixture into a rough dough. Wrap in plastic wrap and refrigerate for 30 minutes.

2. Meanwhile, place the meat in a medium-size bowl, add the soy sauce, ginger, and sesame oil, and mix well with your fingers.

3. Heat a wok or a large heavy skillet over high heat until very hot. Add 1 teaspoon of the corn or canola oil and heat until hot, about 30 seconds. Add the seasoned ground meat and cook over medium-high heat, breaking up any lumps with a spatula, until the meat loses its raw color. Remove and drain in a colander.

4. Reheat the pan over high heat until very hot, add the remaining tablespoon plus 2 teaspoons oil, and heat until hot, about 30 seconds. Add the onions and stir-fry over medium heat until soft and translucent. Add the curry powder and stir-fry until fragrant, about 15 seconds. Add the sauce mixture and cook, stirring constantly,

until it thickens. Add the cooked meat and the peas, toss lightly, and remove the pan from the heat. Spread the filling out on a cookie sheet and refrigerate until cool.

5. Divide the dough in half. On a lightly floured surface, roll one piece of dough out into a circle about ⅛ inch thick. Using a round cookie cutter 2 inches in diameter, cut out circles from the dough and place them on a floured surface. Gather the dough scraps together into a ball, wrap in plastic wrap, and chill for 10 to 15 minutes, while you repeat the process with the remaining dough. Then roll out the chilled scraps and cut more circles; you should have about 36 in all.

6. Preheat the oven to 400 degrees F.

7. Place a heaping teaspoon of the curry filling in the center of each dough circle and fold it over to form a half-circle, enclosing the filling. Use the tines of a fork to create a decorative finish or press and fold to form a pleated finish, on the rounded edge of each turnover.

8. Brush the surface of the turnovers with the beaten egg and bake on greased cookie sheets until golden brown, about 20 minutes. Remove from the oven, let cool briefly, and serve warm.

MAKES ABOUT 36 TURNOVERS

Vegetable Samosas

Traditionally, samosas are deep-fried triangular Indian pastries filled with spicy meat or potatoes, but there are numerous variations all over Asia. I like to use my easy turnover pastry, which is made in the food processor, and bake them, eliminating the deep-frying.

1. Heat a wok or a large heavy skillet over high heat until very hot. Add the cumin seeds and toast until fragrant, about 15 seconds. Add the olive oil and heat until hot, about 30 seconds, then add the onion, ginger, and jalapeño. Cook over medium heat, stirring, until the onion is soft and lightly golden. Add the potatoes and fry until the potatoes become dry, a minute or so. Add the peas and the remaining seasonings, toss lightly to combine, and spoon onto a platter to cool.

2. Divide the dough in half. On a lightly floured surface, roll one piece of dough out to a circle about ⅛ inch thick. Using a round cookie cutter 2 inches in diameter, cut out circles from the dough and place them on a floured surface. Gather the dough scraps together into a ball, wrap in plastic wrap, and chill for 10 to 15 minutes, while you repeat the process with the remaining dough. Then roll out the chilled scraps and cut more circles; you should have about 36 in all.

3. Preheat the oven to 400 degrees F.

4. Place a heaping teaspoon of the potato filling in the center of each dough circle and fold it over to form a half-circle, enclosing the filling. Use the tines of a fork to create a decorative finish or press and fold to form a pleated finish, on the rounded edge of each turnover.

5. Brush the surface of the turnovers with the beaten egg and bake until golden brown, about 20 minutes. Remove from the oven, let cool briefly, and serve warm.

MAKES ABOUT 36 TURNOVERS

FOR THE FILLING:
¾ teaspoon cumin seeds
3 tablespoons olive oil
1 medium-size onion, cut into fine dice (about 1 cup)
2 teaspoons peeled and minced fresh ginger
1 fresh jalapeño pepper, ends trimmed, seeds removed, and chopped (optional)
3 medium-size red potatoes, boiled in water to cover until tender, drained, peeled, and cut into ¼-inch dice
1 cup cooked fresh or frozen peas
1 tablespoon ground coriander
½ teaspoon turmeric
1 teaspoon salt, or to taste

1 recipe Turnover Pastry (page 34), chilled

TO FINISH THE TURNOVERS:
1 large egg, lightly beaten

Vietnamese Spring Rolls

Few appetizers are as appealing as Vietnamese spring rolls, with their delectable stuffing of shrimp, vegetables, and fragrant herbs. I've simplified the filling so they can be made easily. For parties, they can be prepared several hours in advance and covered with a moist towel to prevent the skins from drying out.

3 quarts water

6 ounces thin rice stick noodles or vermicelli, softened in hot water to cover and drained

24 round rice paper wrappers (about 8 inches in diameter)

1½ heads Boston lettuce, cores trimmed, leaves separated, pressed to flatten, rinsed, and drained

2 medium-size carrots, shredded or grated (about 1¼ cups)

¾ cup fresh mint leaves, coarsely shredded

¾ cup cilantro (fresh coriander) leaves, coarsely shredded

¾ pound cooked medium-size shrimp, sliced lengthwise in half

Vietnamese Sweet-and-Sour Dipping Sauce (page 152) or Peanut Sauce (page 147)

1. Heat the water in a large pot until boiling. Add the rice noodles, swish them about, and cook for 1 minute. Drain in a colander, refresh under cold running water, and drain again.

2. Fill a pan with hot water and spread a cotton dish towel out on the work surface. Dip a rice wrapper in the hot water for 3 seconds and spread it out diagonally on the towel. Place a lettuce leaf over the lower third of the rice wrapper. Arrange 2 tablespoons of the rice noodles on top of the lettuce, then add a heaping tablespoon of the carrot shreds, and sprinkle mint and cilantro shreds on top. Fold over the bottom, roll over once to form a cylinder, folding in the two sides to form a neat package. Arrange two shrimp halves, cut side down, in a row across the wrapper and continue rolling up into a tight cylindrical shape. Place the finished roll on a serving platter and cover with a damp dish towel to prevent it from drying out. Repeat with the remaining wrappers and filling ingredients.

3. Serve the rolls with the sauce of your choice for dipping.

MAKES 24 ROLLS

Fresh Chinese Spring Rolls

Fresh spring rolls, such as these, are often prepared for the "cold foods" festival in the spring, a holiday that honors dead ancestors. They are delightful year-round. Myriad stir-fried meat, seafood, and vegetable mixtures are wrapped in paper-thin spring roll skins and eaten hot or at room temperature.

24 spring roll skins (also labeled "lumpia" wrappers) or flour tortillas
Toasted sesame oil as needed
2 tablespoons safflower or corn oil

FOR THE SEASONINGS:
2½ tablespoons minced garlic
2 tablespoons peeled and minced fresh ginger
10 dried Chinese black mushrooms, softened in hot water to cover, drained, stems removed, and caps shredded

FOR THE FILLING:
3 cups shredded and well-washed leeks (white section only)
2 cups grated carrots
5 cups cored and finely shredded Chinese (Napa) cabbage
1½ tablespoons rice wine or sake
4 cups bean sprouts, rinsed and drained

FOR THE SAUCE, mixed together:
3 tablespoons soy sauce
1½ teaspoons toasted sesame oil

¼ teaspoon freshly ground black pepper
½ teaspoon cornstarch

TO SERVE:
½ cup hoisin sauce, heated with 3 tablespoons water and placed in a serving bowl

1. Separate the spring roll skins or flour tortillas and lightly brush with sesame oil. Fold in half, arrange on a rack in a steamer filled with boiling water, and steam for 5 minutes. Keep warm in a basket covered with a towel.

2. Heat a wok or a large heavy skillet over high heat until very hot. Add the oil and heat until hot, about 30 seconds. Add the seasonings and stir-fry for about 10 seconds. Add the leeks and stir-fry for about 1 minute, then add the carrots, cabbage, and rice wine and cook, tossing until the vegetables are crisp-tender. Add the bean sprouts and sauce mixture and cook, stirring, until thickened. Transfer to a serving platter.

3. To eat, smear a spring roll skin or tortilla with a dollop of the hoisin mixture, arrange some of the stir-fried vegetable mixture on top, roll up, and eat with your fingers.

MAKES 24 ROLLS

Cantonese Spring Rolls

With their sumptuous filling of shredded pork, shrimp, black mushrooms, and garlic chives and their delicate, lacy flour-and-water wrappers, these spring rolls are irresistible. Invite some friends over to help and make a double batch. Once cooked, they freeze and reheat beautifully.

1 pound sirloin or center-cut pork fillets, trimmed of fat and gristle

FOR THE MARINADE, mixed together:
1 tablespoon soy sauce
2 tablespoons rice wine or sake
½ teaspoon toasted sesame oil
1½ teaspoons cornstarch

FOR THE FILLING:
⅓ pound raw medium-size shrimp, peeled, deveined, rinsed, drained, and patted dry
1 tablespoon plus 1 teaspoon peeled and minced fresh ginger
1 tablespoon rice wine or sake
1 teaspoon cornstarch
7 tablespoons safflower or corn oil
1 tablespoon minced garlic
10 dried Chinese black mushrooms, softened in hot water to cover, drained, stems removed, and caps shredded
4 cups thin julienne strips cored Chinese (Napa) cabbage
2 cups fresh Chinese garlic chives or leeks (white section only), cut into 1-inch lengths
2 cups bean sprouts, rinsed and drained

FOR THE SAUCE, mixed together:
2 tablespoons soy sauce
2 tablespoons rice wine or sake
1 teaspoon toasted sesame oil
¼ teaspoon freshly ground black pepper
½ teaspoon cornstarch

TO MAKE AND FRY THE ROLLS:
30 spring roll skins (also labeled "lumpia" wrappers)
6 tablespoons water
3 tablespoons all-purpose flour
4 cups safflower or corn oil

TO SERVE:
Chinese plum or duck sauce
Chinese hot mustard

1. Using a sharp knife, cut the pork across the grain into paper-thin slices, then cut the slices into matchstick-size shreds. Place in a medium-size bowl, add the marinade, toss lightly to coat, and let marinate for 20 minutes at room temperature. Drain.

2. Slice the shrimp lengthwise in half. Cut into ¼-inch dice. Place in a small bowl, add 1 teaspoon of the minced ginger, the rice wine, and cornstarch, and toss lightly to coat.

3. Heat a wok or a large heavy skillet over high heat until very hot. Add 3 tablespoons of the oil and heat until hot, about 30 seconds. Add the drained pork and stir-fry, stirring constantly, until the meat loses its pink color and separates into shreds. Remove with a handled strainer or a slotted spoon and drain in a colander.

Wipe out the pan. Reheat the pan, add 2 tablespoons of the oil, and heat until hot over high heat. Add the shrimp and stir-fry until opaque. Remove with a handled strainer or a slotted spoon and drain in a colander. Wipe out the pan.

4. Reheat the pan, add the remaining 2 tablespoons oil, and heat until hot over high heat. Add the remaining 1 tablespoon minced ginger, the garlic, and mushrooms and stir-fry until fragrant, about 15 seconds. Add the cabbage and toss lightly over high heat until slightly limp, about 1½ minutes. Add the garlic chives or leeks and the bean sprouts, toss lightly for 30 seconds, and add the sauce mixture. Cook, stirring continuously to prevent lumps, until thickened. Transfer to a serving platter to cool. Clean out the pan.

5. Separate the spring roll skins and cover them with a damp cotton dish towel to keep them from drying out. In a small bowl, mix the water and flour together until smooth. Arrange a skin facing you. Squeeze a heaping tablespoon of the filling to remove any excess liquid and place toward the lower third of the wrapper. Roll up to form a cylindrical shape, folding in the two sides as you roll. Spread some of the flour mixture on the top edge and press to seal the seam. Repeat with the remaining wrappers and filling.

6. Reheat the wok or skillet over high heat until very hot. Add the oil and heat to 375 degrees F. Add a batch of the spring rolls without crowding them, and fry, turning constantly so they cook evenly, until golden brown and crisp. Remove with a handled strainer or a slotted spoon and drain on paper towels. (You may want to keep them warm in a preheated 250-degree-F oven.) Reheat the oil until hot again and continue frying the remaining rolls in batches, reheating the oil each time. Serve with the plum sauce and hot mustard. (You can freeze the rolls once they have cooled. To serve, defrost, arrange on a rack placed on a baking sheet, and reheat in a preheated 375-degree-F oven until crisp, about 15 minutes.)

MAKES 30 ROLLS

Crisp Vietnamese Shrimp Fingers with Fresh Herbs

Shrimp paste, redolent of fresh ginger and scallions, is a versatile mixture. It can be shaped into balls, spread on bread, or piped onto wonton skins and fried until golden brown, as in this recipe.

⅔ pound medium-size raw shrimp, peeled, deveined, rinsed, drained, and patted dry

½ cup canned whole water chestnuts, blanched in boiling water for 10 seconds, refreshed under cold running water, drained, blotted dry, and chopped

FOR THE SEASONINGS, mixed together:
1½ tablespoons peeled and minced fresh ginger

1½ tablespoons minced scallion whites

1½ tablespoons rice wine or sake

1 teaspoon toasted sesame oil

¾ teaspoon salt

1 large egg white, lightly beaten

2 tablespoons cornstarch

TO FORM AND FRY THE ROLLS:
25 wonton skins

1 large egg, lightly beaten

4 cups safflower or corn oil

TO SERVE:
2 heads Boston lettuce, cores trimmed, leaves separated, pressed to flatten, rinsed, drained, and arranged in a basket or a bowl

Vietnamese Sweet-and-Sour Dipping Sauce (page 152)

1 cup fresh basil leaves, cut into fine shreds and placed in a small bowl

1. Place the shrimp in a food processor fitted with the steel blade and process into a paste. Transfer to a large bowl, add the water chestnuts and seasonings, and stir vigorously in one direction until the mixture forms a stiff paste. Refrigerate, if possible, for 2 hours so that the mixture becomes firm.

2. Fill a pastry bag without a tip with the shrimp mixture. (Alternatively, you can use a spoon.) Spread out wonton wrappers on a counter. (Keep the unused skins covered with a damp dish towel to prevent them from drying out.) Pipe a strip of the shrimp paste ¼ inch in from the edge, running from top to bottom, of one wrapper. Using your finger or a brush, spread a little beaten egg along the opposite edge. Roll over the skin to enclose the shrimp paste and continue rolling to form a cylinder. Press lightly to seal the seam. Don't roll too tightly, or the skin will split while frying. Repeat with the remaining filling and skins.

3. Heat a wok or a large heavy skillet over high heat until very hot. Add the oil and heat to 375 degrees F. Deep-fry the shrimp rolls in batches without crowding, turning constantly, until golden brown, 3 to 4 minutes. Remove with a handled strainer or slotted spoon and drain briefly in a colander, then transfer to paper towels.

4. Arrange the rolls on a serving platter and serve with the dipping sauce. To eat, sprinkle some basil on a lettuce leaf, roll up a shrimp finger in the lettuce, and eat with your fingers. (The rolls can be reheated in a preheated 375-degree-F oven until crisp and piping hot, about 10 minutes.)

MAKES 25 ROLLS

Lotus Chicken Packages

One of my favorite Cantonese *dim sum* are these fragrant steamed packages stuffed with sticky rice and chicken with black mushrooms. You can add all kinds of savory delicacies. Many Cantonese favor sausage and quail's egg, but I make a simplified version that's heady with ginger and garlic.

2 cups uncooked sweet (glutinous) rice
3 dried lotus leaves (see Note)
¾ pound boned chicken breast meat, skin removed

FOR THE CHICKEN MARINADE:
2 tablespoons soy sauce
1 tablespoon rice wine
1 teaspoon sesame oil
1 teaspoon minced garlic
1 teaspoon peeled and minced fresh ginger

FOR THE RICE SEASONINGS:
1½ tablespoons soy sauce
1 tablespoon rice wine or sake
1 teaspoon toasted sesame oil
½ teaspoon salt

3 tablespoons safflower or corn oil
8 dried Chinese black mushrooms, soaked in hot water to cover for 20 minutes, stems removed and caps diced

FOR THE CHICKEN SAUCE:
¼ cup chicken broth or water
2 tablespoons soy sauce
1 tablespoon rice wine or sake
1½ teaspoons cornstarch
¼ teaspoon ground black pepper

1. Using your hands as a rake, rinse the rice under cold running water until the water runs clear. Drain and place in cold water to cover. Soak for 1 hour. Place the lotus leaves in hot water to cover for 1 hour. Line a steamer tray with wet cheesecloth or parchment paper punched with holes and transfer the rice to the steamer tray, distributing it evenly. Cover and steam the rice for 20 minutes over high heat. Remove and keep covered.

2. Trim away any fat or gristle from the chicken and cut the meat into 1-inch cubes. Place in a bowl, add the chicken marinade, toss lightly to coat, and let marinate for 20 minutes. Drain and cut each lotus leaf in half at the natural division.

3. Transfer the cooked rice to a mixing bowl and add the rice seasonings. Toss lightly to combine.

4. Heat a wok, add the oil, and heat until very hot. Add the chicken and stir-fry over high heat until the meat changes color. Remove with a handled strainer or slotted spoon, and drain. Reheat the wok, add the black mushrooms, chicken, and chicken sauce. Stir-fry over high heat until the sauce has thickened, stirring constantly to prevent lumps. Remove and let cool. Separate into 6 portions.

5. Place a lotus-leaf half on the counter, right side down. The rounded edge should be up. Spoon some of the rice mixture into the center and, using a spoon dipped in water, shape into a rounded circle, making an indentation in the center. Fill with a portion of the chicken mixture. Using more rice to cover, form into a stuffed circle. Fold in the edges of the leaf and fold down the top and bottom to form a square package. Tie securely with twine. Repeat to make 6 packages. Arrange the packages in the steamer tray. Cover.

6. Fill a wok or a pot with water level with the bottom of the steamer tray and heat until boiling. Place the steamer tray over the boiling water and steam, covered, for 25 minutes over high heat. Remove and untie the twine. Arrange the packages on a platter and serve. Before eating, open each package and discard the leaves. To reheat the packages, steam for 10 minutes.

MAKES 6 SERVINGS

Note: If lotus leaves are unavailable, cut parchment paper into 6-inch squares and use as the wrappers, securing the packages with kitchen twine.

Basic Sushi

Sushi has become the quintessential Japanese dish, but the modern sushi bar as we know it, with dexterous chefs masterfully preparing rolls of vinegared rice with fresh seafood and vegetables, didn't appear in Japan until 1926. Originally, sushi was a pickle made with fermented fish or clams. Happily, because of its tremendous popularity, there are now numerous variations and shapes. This is one of the most basic types of sushi and one of the easiest to prepare at home.

7 dried Chinese black mushrooms, softened in 1 cup hot water for 20 minutes
6 tablespoons soy sauce
¼ cup sugar

FOR THE RICE:
2 cups short-grain or Japanese rice
2 cups plus 2 tablespoons water

FOR THE RICE SEASONINGS, mixed together to dissolve the sugar:
¼ cup Japanese rice vinegar
2 tablespoons sugar
½ teaspoon salt

FOR THE VEGETABLES:
3 medium-size carrots, cut into julienne strips about 2 inches long and ¼ inch thick
½ pound fresh spinach, stems removed, well rinsed, and drained

FOR THE ROLLS:
Rice vinegar as needed
6 sheets nori seaweed, toasted briefly over an open flame on one side

TO SERVE:
Pickled ginger
Soy sauce
Wasabi

1. Drain the mushrooms, reserving the liquid. Remove the stems and discard. Cut the caps into julienne strips about ¼ inch thick. Place the mushrooms in a small heavy saucepan with the reserved liquid, the soy sauce, and sugar. Bring to a boil, reduce the heat to a simmer, and cook until the mushrooms have absorbed all the liquid. Remove from the heat.

2. Put the rice in a medium-size bowl and, using your fingers as a rake, rinse the rice under cold running water to remove some of the talc. Drain the rice in a colander. Put the rice and water in a heavy 2-quart saucepan with a lid. Heat, uncovered, until boiling. Reduce the heat to low, cover tightly, and simmer for about 15 minutes. Remove the pan from the heat and let sit until the water has evaporated and craters appear in the surface, about 5 minutes. Fluff lightly with a fork to separate the grains, then add the rice seasonings and mix evenly with a wooden spatula. Spread the hot rice out on a tray and fan it to cool it more quickly. (This will give it a sheen and prevent it from being sticky or gummy.)

3. Cook the carrot strips in boiling water to cover until just tender, about 10 minutes. Refresh under cold running water and drain. Blanch the spinach in boiling water for 5 seconds, refresh under cold running water, and squeeze dry. Drain on paper towels.

4. Prepare a bowl of water with some rice vinegar in it for rinsing your hands and keeping the rice from sticking to your hands. Place a *sudare* (bamboo rolling mat) or a sheet of heavy-duty aluminum foil on the counter. Place a piece of the nori, toasted side up, on the mat or foil about ¼ inch from the edge closest to you.

5. With your hands or a wooden spoon, spread a generous ⅓ cup of the seasoned rice on the nori in an even layer, leaving a 1-inch border across the top at the farthest edge. Brush the border with a little water right before sealing to help make it stick.

6. Using a chopstick or your hands, make a shallow groove across the middle of the rice. Arrange one sixth of the mushrooms, carrots, and spinach in the groove.

7. Using the *sudare* or aluminum foil, roll up the nori and rice, jelly-roll-style, into a compact roll. Lightly squeeze the mat or foil with your hands to make a firm roll and seal the edge by pressing the nori together. With a sharp knife that has been moistened with a damp cloth, trim the ends of the roll to even them and cut the roll into ½-inch-thick slices, cleaning the knife between slices. Repeat with the remaining nori, rice, and vegetables.

8. Arrange the sushi on a serving plate and serve with pickled ginger and soy sauce flavored with a dash of wasabi for dipping.

MAKES 6 SERVINGS

Hand-Rolled Sushi with Smoked Salmon

Rolled sushi, or *maki-sushi,* such as this is most frequently wrapped in seaweed, or *nori,* but other ingredients such as thin omelets and tofu are also traditionally used. As sushi chefs do, I like to improvise, using whatever ingredients are available. This delicious sushi is easy and it can be prepared several hours in advance and refrigerated until ready to serve.

Rice vinegar as needed

1 pound thinly sliced smoked salmon

4½ cups cooked short-grain or Japanese rice with rice seasonings, prepared as directed in step 2, Basic Sushi (page 48)

6 tablespoons capers, drained

½ red onion, cut into thin slices

TO SERVE:

Smoked Salmon Sushi Dipping Sauce (optional; page 150)

1. Prepare a bowl of water with some rice vinegar in it for rinsing your hands and keeping the rice from sticking to your hands. Spread a *sudare* (bamboo rolling mat) on a counter. Place a sheet of plastic wrap about the same size as the mat on top of it. Using one sixth of the salmon, arrange overlapping slices of the smoked salmon on the plastic wrap to form an 8-inch square. Spread a generous ¾ cup of the vinegared rice evenly over the salmon, leaving a ½- to ¾-inch border at the far edge of the square. Using a chopstick, make a shallow groove across the middle of the rice. Sprinkle 1 tablespoon of the rinsed capers and a line of the red onion slices in the groove.

2. Picking up the edge of the rolling mat and plastic wrap closest to you, roll the salmon and rice up, jelly-roll-style to form a compact roll. Press in the rice at the ends and lightly squeeze with the mat and wrap so that it is a firm roll. With a sharp knife, trim the ends to even them and cut the roll, on the diagonal or straight, into ½-inch-thick slices. Repeat with the remaining salmon, rice, capers, and onions.

3. Arrange the sushi on a serving plate and serve with the dipping sauce, if desired.

Alternative rolling method: Cut each salmon slice in half lengthwise. Arrange a 10-inch square of heavy-duty aluminum foil on the counter. Lay a piece of salmon on top. Sprinkle some of the capers and red onion shreds on the salmon. Grab about 1½ tablespoons of the seasoned rice and shape it into an oval. Place across one end of the salmon slice and roll up the salmon, using the aluminum foil, so that the salmon encloses the rice. Arrange on a serving plate. Repeat the procedure with the remaining salmon slices, capers, onions, and rice. Serve with the dipping sauce.

MAKES 6 SERVINGS

Salads in a Wrap

VIETNAMESE CHICKEN SALAD ❧ CURRIED CHICKEN SALAD WITH GRAPES ❧ SESAME CHICKEN SALAD ❧ VIETNAMESE FRESH MINT SALAD ❧ LEMONY THAI SALAD PACKAGES ❧ HOT-AND-SOUR SLAW WITH SHRIMP ❧ SEAFOOD RICE BUNDLES ❧ SOBA BUNDLES WITH CHILI-GARLIC DRESSING ❧ INDONESIAN SALAD WITH COCONUT-PEANUT DRESSING ❧ SAUCY VEGETABLE ROLL-UPS

I would never want to have to choose my favorite variety of roll-up or wrap, but salads are definitely one of my favorites. They are so sensual, with their different textures: the crisp vegetables contrasted with the tender slices of cooked meat or seafood, all brought together in the mouth with a fresh, light dressing. And they offer infinite opportunities for improvisation.

Take, for instance, the classic Indonesian salad with *gado-gado* sauce: This dish is a marvelous intermingling of Eastern and Western ingredients, with potatoes and string beans as well as tofu and bean sprouts all smothered in a velvety coconut-peanut sauce and wrapped up by the handful in iceberg lettuce leaves. Then there's the sumptuous Korean salad of cooked chicken, shredded cucumber and carrots, and delicate angel hair noodles tossed in a toasted sesame dressing redolent of garlic and chili paste. It's served in wedges of golden egg crêpes.

These are not ordinary salads but a diverse mixture of Eastern and Western ideas. I like to make a warm wilted hot-and-sour cabbage slaw embellished with shrimp and served in red-tipped or plain leafy lettuce. Cold nutty soba noodles are sprinkled with slivered leeks, red bell peppers, and bean sprouts, then tossed in a chili-garlic sauce and served in blanched Napa cabbage leaves. There's even a chicken-and-grape salad tossed with a deliciously creamy curried yogurt dressing and served in Bibb lettuce.

Perhaps more than any other chapter in this book, these recipes reflect my love for experimenting with the offerings in the produce section. Never before has there been such a wonderful or expansive selection of fresh vegetables to choose from. Just look at the salad greens: Where there once was only a meager display of iceberg lettuce, there now is a veritable treasure trove of different greens, including arugula; chicory; Bibb, Boston, red leaf, and butter lettuce; escarole; radicchio; romaine; spinach; and watercress. Even cabbages are more interesting: bok choy, Napa, and Savoy in addition to the familiar red and green cabbage. The list is almost endless and each green—which I mix and match for the wrappers—offers its own fine flavor and texture to the dish.

Enjoy these different salads and know that with each delicious bite you're giving your body a generous dose of good health.

Vietnamese Chicken Salad

With their fresh, lively seasonings and contrasting textures of tender meat or seafood, sensual cooked noodles, and crisp vegetables, Vietnamese salads are superb as a light but filling lunch or dinner. Traditionally, they are served in rice noodle wrappers, but I much prefer to serve them rolled in Boston or Bibb lettuce.

1. In a large pot, heat the water until boiling. Add the softened rice stick noodles and swirl in the hot water, then cook until just tender, 10 to 15 seconds. Drain thoroughly in a colander and rinse under cold running water. Clip the noodles into 3-inch lengths, if desired, and arrange on a deep serving platter.

2. Arrange the chicken in the center of the platter over the noodles and then arrange the carrots and bean sprouts around it in concentric circles.

3. Sprinkle the cilantro, basil, scallions, and chopped peanuts on top of the salad. Serve the salad at room temperature or chilled. You can serve the dressing on the side as a dipping sauce or pour it over the top and toss before serving. To eat the salad, spoon some of the salad mixture into a lettuce leaf, roll it up, tucking in the sides, and eat with your fingers.

MAKES 6 SERVINGS

2 quarts water
½ pound thin rice stick noodles, softened in hot water to cover and drained
1¼ pounds cooked chicken, skin removed, shredded by hand into julienne strips
2 medium-size carrots, grated (about 1½ cups)
2 cups bean sprouts, rinsed and drained
¼ cup coarsely chopped cilantro (fresh coriander) leaves
¼ cup coarsely chopped fresh basil leaves
½ cup finely chopped scallion greens
¼ cup chopped dry-roasted peanuts

TO SERVE:
Vietnamese Sweet-and-Sour Dipping Sauce (page 152)
2 to 3 heads Boston lettuce, cores trimmed, leaves separated, pressed to flatten, rinsed, drained, and arranged on a serving platter or in a basket

Curried Chicken Salad with Grapes

I have never been quiet about my disdain for chicken salad with grapes, but the idea for this salad roll-up was so appealing that I was determined to set aside my previous feelings. (Forgive me, Michele.) What makes this salad so special is that the pungent curry seasonings are beautifully complemented by the sweet red grapes.

2 whole boneless, skinless chicken breasts, fat removed

3 slices fresh ginger with skin, smashed lightly with the flat side of a cleaver

3 tablespoons rice wine or sake

3 to 4 stalks celery, ends trimmed and thinly sliced (about 2 cups)

½ pound green or red seedless grapes or apples, cored, diced, and sprinkled with lemon juice

3 tablespoons chopped scallion greens

FOR THE CURRIED YOGURT DRESSING, ground to a paste and mixed in a food processor:

One 1½-inch piece fresh ginger, peeled and cut into 4 slices

2 cloves garlic, peeled

1½ teaspoons curry powder, preferably Madras curry

¾ cup plain low-fat yogurt

½ teaspoon salt

¼ teaspoon freshly ground black pepper

TO SERVE:

2 heads Bibb lettuce, cores trimmed, leaves separated, pressed to flatten, rinsed, drained, and arranged around the rim of a large bowl or serving dish

1. Put the chicken breasts, ginger slices, rice wine, and water to cover in a medium-size saucepan and heat until boiling. Reduce the heat to medium and simmer, uncovered, until the breasts are cooked, about 12 minutes. Remove the chicken and let cool, reserving the broth for another use. Cut the chicken into ½-inch dice.

2. Mix together the chicken, celery, grapes or apples, and scallions in a large bowl and add the curry dressing. Toss to coat. Portion the chicken salad in the center of the lettuce leaves and serve. To eat, spoon some of the salad onto a leaf, roll it up, tucking in the sides, and eat with your fingers.

MAKES 6 SERVINGS

Sesame Chicken Salad

Toasted sesame seeds and scallions, traditional Korean seasonings, give this appealing salad a distinctive flavor. Healthy doses of chili paste and rice vinegar further enliven the dish. Traditionally, the egg pancakes are cut into shreds and sprinkled on the salad. I like to quarter them and use them as wrappers to hold mouthfuls of the seasoned vegetables.

3 quarts water

⅓ pound thin egg noodles, such as angel hair or vermicelli

2 medium-size carrots, grated or shredded (about 1½ cups)

2 English seedless cucumbers, ends trimmed, halved lengthwise, seeded, grated or shredded, and squeezed to remove excess water (about 2 cups)

Korean Sesame Dressing (page 154)

1 pound cooked chicken, skin removed and cut or shredded by hand into thin julienne strips

TO SERVE:

1 teaspoon safflower or corn oil

5 large eggs, lightly beaten with 2 tablespoons water and ½ teaspoon salt

½ cup finely minced scallion greens

1. Bring the water to a boil in a large pot. Add the noodles and cook until just tender, 3 to 5 minutes. Drain in a colander, rinse under cold running water, and drain again.

2. Toss the noodles, carrots, cucumbers, and half of the sesame dressing in a large bowl. Arrange on a serving platter or a bowl, leaving a space in the center for the chicken. Arrange the chicken in the center.

3. With a paper towel dipped in the oil, wipe the inside of a 9- or 10-inch nonstick frying pan. Heat over medium-high heat until hot (a little water sprinkled on it should evaporate immediately). Ladle ¼ cup of the beaten eggs into the pan and tilt the pan to form a thin circle of egg. Cook briefly until set, about 10 seconds. Flip over using a spatula and cook very briefly on the other side. Remove and let cool, stacking the pancakes on a plate as you cook the remaining egg. There should be about 7 pancakes. Cut them into quarters and arrange them around the outer edge of the serving platter.

4. Pour the remaining dressing over the chicken and sprinkle with the minced scallions. To eat, spoon some of the noodles and chicken onto an egg pancake, roll up, tucking in the edges, and eat with your fingers.

MAKES 6 SERVINGS

Vietnamese Fresh Mint Salad

I had become enraptured with the fresh, vibrant flavorings and sensuous textures of Vietnamese cooking long before I visited Hanoi and Ho Chi Minh City. These compelling characteristics are especially apparent in salads such as this one. I substitute lean ground turkey for the traditional pork or beef, as a healthful alternative.

1 cup Japanese rice vinegar
¼ cup sugar
1½ medium-size red onions, cut into small dice (about 2½ cups)
3 medium-size carrots, grated or shredded (about 3½ cups)
1¼ pounds ground turkey
1 stalk lemongrass, ends trimmed, tough outer leaves removed, cut into 2-inch lengths, and minced in a food processor or blender (if unavailable, substitute the grated zest of 1 lemon)
1½ tablespoons fish sauce
2 teaspoons safflower or corn oil

FOR THE VIETNAMESE DRESSING, mixed together:
2 small fresh red chili peppers, ends trimmed, seeds removed, and cut into fine julienne shreds
3 tablespoons minced garlic
½ cup fish sauce
5½ tablespoons sugar, or more to taste
3½ tablespoons chopped fresh mint leaves
3½ tablespoons chopped fresh basil leaves

TO SERVE:
2 heads Boston or leafy lettuce, cores trimmed, leaves separated, pressed to flatten, rinsed, drained, and arranged around the rim of a serving platter

1. Pour the rice vinegar and sugar in a bowl and stir to dissolve the sugar. Place the onions and carrots in the bowl and let sit for 15 to 20 minutes.

2. Mix together the ground turkey, lemongrass, and fish sauce in a large bowl.

3. Heat a wok or a large heavy skillet over high heat until very hot. Add the oil and heat until hot, about 30 seconds. Add the turkey mixture and stir-fry over medium-high heat, mashing to break up any clumps of meat, until the meat changes color and separates. Drain in a colander and wipe out the pan.

4. Using a slotted spoon, remove the carrots and onions from the vinegar, draining well, and arrange them on the serving platter, leaving a slight well in the center for the cooked turkey. Add the vinegar from the carrots and onions to the dressing. Spoon the cooked meat into the center of the vegetables and sprinkle the fresh herbs on top. Just before serving, pour the dressing over the salad and toss lightly. To eat, spoon some of the salad onto a lettuce leaf, roll it up, tucking in the sides, and eat with your fingers. (You may fold the package into a roll and secure with a garlic chive, as illustrated.)

MAKES 6 SERVINGS

Lemony Thai Salad Packages

In Thailand, no part of the cilantro plant is wasted. The root is used in marinades, while the stems and leaves are used in dressings. Here's my interpretation of a delicious Thai salad, liberally seasoned with cilantro, lemon, crushed red pepper, and garlic. You can substitute chicken or turkey for the pork.

1½ pounds sirloin or center-cut pork fillets, trimmed of fat and gristle

FOR THE MARINADE, blended to a paste in a food processor or blender:

4 cloves garlic, peeled

1 teaspoon crushed red pepper

2 tablespoons rice wine or sake

1 tablespoon finely chopped cilantro (fresh coriander) root or stem

1 tablespoon sugar

¼ cup fish sauce

1 tablespoon toasted sesame oil

FOR THE BEAN SPROUTS:

1 teaspoon safflower or corn oil

2 cups minced scallion greens

5 cups bean sprouts, rinsed and drained

2 tablespoons rice wine or sake

FOR THE LEMONY SAUCE, mixed together to dissolve the sugar:

5½ tablespoons fish sauce

¼ cup freshly squeezed lemon juice or juice of 1 lime

1½ tablespoons firmly packed light brown sugar

½ teaspoon freshly ground black pepper

¼ cup chopped cilantro (fresh coriander) leaves

½ cup coarsely chopped dry-roasted peanuts

TO SERVE:

1 large head romaine lettuce, core trimmed, leaves separated, pressed to flatten, rinsed, drained, and arranged on a serving platter or in a basket

1. In a large bowl, mix the pork and marinade together, tossing to coat. Cover with plastic wrap and let stand at room temperature for 2 hours.

2. Prepare a medium-hot fire for grilling or preheat the broiler. Arrange the meat 3 inches from the source of heat and grill or broil for about 10 minutes per side (about 12 minutes per side for thicker cuts). Remove, let cool slightly, and cut on the diagonal into slices about ⅛ inch thick and 3 inches long.

3. While the pork is cooking, heat a wok or a large heavy skillet over high heat until very hot. Add the safflower or corn oil and heat until very hot. Add the scallions and stir-fry until fragrant, about 30 seconds, then add the bean sprouts and rice wine and stir-fry for about 1 minute. Remove and spoon into a serving bowl.

4. Arrange the grilled meat over the bean sprouts. Drizzle the lemony sauce on top. Sprinkle the peanuts on top. To eat, spoon some of the pork and bean sprouts into a lettuce leaf, roll up, tucking in the sides, and eat with your fingers.

MAKES 6 SERVINGS

Hot-and-Sour Slaw with Shrimp

Hot-and-sour is a popular theme in Asian cooking. Here, crisp-cooked cabbage and carrots with shrimp are tossed in a pungent dressing liberally laced with hot chili peppers and mellow black vinegar. You can tone down the flavor to your own taste. I often experiment with different types of cabbage, substituting Savoy and white cabbage for the Napa.

1 pound cooked medium-size
    shrimp, peeled
1 medium-size head Chinese
    (Napa) cabbage (about
    1 pound), leaves separated,
    stems trimmed, rinsed, and
    drained
1 teaspoon salt
2 teaspoons canola or corn oil
1 teaspoon toasted sesame oil
1 teaspoon crushed red pepper,
    or to taste
2½ tablespoons peeled and
    minced fresh ginger

1 medium-size red bell pepper,
    cored, seeded, and cut into
    ¼-inch dice
1½ tablespoons rice wine or sake
4 medium-size carrots, finely
    shredded or grated (about
    4 cups)

FOR THE HOT-AND-SOUR DRESSING,
    mixed together:
¼ cup soy sauce
½ teaspoon salt
3 tablespoons sugar
3 tablespoons Chinese black
    vinegar or Worcestershire sauce

TO SERVE:
2 heads red leaf or plain leafy
    lettuce, cores trimmed, leaves
    separated, pressed to flatten,
    rinsed, drained, and arranged
    on a serving platter or in a
    basket

1. Using a sharp knife, slice the shrimp in half down the back.

2. With a sharp knife, cut the cabbage leaves into thin julienne shreds. Place the shreds in a bowl, add the salt, toss lightly, and let sit for 30 minutes. Using your hands, squeeze the excess water from the cabbage.

3. Heat a wok or a large heavy skillet over high heat until very hot. Add the oils and heat until hot. Add the crushed red pepper and minced ginger and stir-fry for about 10 seconds. Add the red pepper dice and rice wine and stir-fry for about a minute. Add the cabbage and stir-fry for 15 to 20 seconds, then add the carrots and toss to mix. Add the dressing, then add the cooked shrimp, tossing lightly to coat, and transfer to a serving bowl.

4. Serve the salad warm, at room temperature, or cold. To eat, spoon some of the shrimp slaw mixture on top of a lettuce leaf, roll up, and eat with your fingers.

MAKES 6 SERVINGS

Seafood Rice Bundles

Rice salad is a versatile medium for numerous garnishes. I love to mix and match cooked seafood, meats, and vegetables, depending on what is in season or happens to be in my refrigerator. I also vary the fresh herbs in the vinaigrette dressing to suit the ingredients. Since cilantro has a delicious affinity for seafood, it's wonderful in this salad. Feel free to substitute other fresh herbs as your mood or the occasion dictates.

¾ pound medium-size raw shrimp, shelled, deveined, and rinsed

¾ pound sea scallops, rinsed, drained, and sliced in half through the thickness

FOR THE SEAFOOD MARINADE, mixed together:

3 tablespoons soy sauce

1½ teaspoons toasted sesame oil

½ cup rice wine or sake

3 tablespoons peeled and minced fresh ginger

Twenty 10-inch-long bamboo skewers, soaked in cold water for 1 hour and drained

TO FINISH THE SALAD:

½ pound snow or snap peas, ends snapped and veiny strings removed

4 cups cold cooked jasmine or basmati rice

1 small red onion, cut into small dice (about 1 cup)

1 medium-size red bell pepper, cored, seeded, and cut into small dice

1 medium-size yellow bell pepper, cored, seeded, and cut into small dice

Fresh Cilantro Vinaigrette (page 157)

TO SERVE:

2 heads Bibb or Boston lettuce, cores trimmed, leaves separated, pressed to flatten, rinsed, drained, and arranged on a serving platter

1. In separate bowls, toss the shrimp and scallops with half the marinade each. Let sit for 20 minutes. Thread the shrimp and scallops separately onto skewers.

2. Prepare a medium-hot fire for grilling or preheat the broiler.

3. Blanch the snow peas in boiling water for 5 seconds, refresh under cold running water, drain, and dry on paper towels. Cut crosswise in half.

4. Grill or broil the seafood until cooked through, 4 to 5 minutes on each side. Remove from the skewers and place in a large bowl. Add the cooked rice, snow peas, onion, bell peppers, and vinaigrette and toss lightly to mix. Portion onto a serving platter and chill, or serve at room temperature.

5. To eat, spoon some of the seafood rice mixture onto a lettuce leaf, roll up, tucking in the edges, and eat with your fingers.

MAKES 6 SERVINGS

Soba Bundles with Chili-Garlic Dressing

I have adored the nutty flavor of soba noodles since I sampled them on my first trip to Japan in the seventies. Years later, when I was developing recipes for my *Asian Noodles* book, I began to fully understand their versatility: They are delicious served hot in soups, stir-fried, or served cold in salads, as in this dish.

1 pound firm tofu, cut through the thickness into ½-inch-thick slices

FOR THE SAUCY MARINADE, mixed together:

½ cup hoisin sauce
1½ tablespoons ketchup
1 tablespoon soy sauce
1 tablespoon minced garlic

TO FINISH:

3 quarts water
1 head Savoy or Chinese (Napa) cabbage, leaves rinsed and separated, pressed to flatten, and stems trimmed
6 ounces soba noodles
2 teaspoons safflower or corn oil
2 leeks, trimmed down to the white and 1 inch of the green, split lengthwise, well washed, and cut into thin shreds about 1 inch long (about 2½ cups)
2 medium-size red bell peppers, cored, seeded, and cut into thin julienne strips
1½ tablespoons rice wine or sake
3 cups bean sprouts, rinsed and drained
Chili-Garlic Dressing (page 155)

1. Wrap the tofu slices in paper towels or a cotton dish towel and place a heavy weight, such as a cast-iron skillet, on top. Let stand for 30 minutes to press out the excess water.

2. Preheat the oven to 375 degrees F.

3. Cut the pressed tofu into ¼-inch-thick slices and toss with the marinade. Arrange the slices on a cookie sheet that has been lined with aluminum foil. Bake for 30 minutes, turning once. Cool slightly. Cut into sticks that are 1 inch long and ¼ inch thick.

4. In a large pot, bring the water to a boil. Add the cabbage leaves and blanch for 4 seconds. Remove from the water and refresh under cold running water. Drain thoroughly on paper towels and arrange around the edges of a serving platter.

5. Bring the water back to a boil. Add the soba noodles and stir to separate. Once the water reaches a boil, turn the heat down to medium and cook until just tender, about 3½ minutes. Drain in a colander and rinse under cold running water. Drain again.

6. Heat a wok or a large heavy skillet over high heat until very hot. Add the oil and heat until hot. Add the leeks, red peppers, and rice wine and stir-fry until just tender, about 1 minute. Add the bean sprouts and chili-garlic dressing and toss lightly. Add the tofu and soba and toss lightly to coat and mix together. Spoon over the cabbage. To eat, spoon some of the soba mixture onto a cabbage leaf, roll up, tucking in the edges, and eat with your fingers.

MAKES 6 SERVINGS

Indonesian Salad with Coconut-Peanut Dressing

This unique salad, called *gado gado*, illustrates the blending of Eastern and Western cultures, with its use of Asian and European vegetables. *Gado gado* is a sumptuous spread that usually includes tofu, string beans, cauliflower, and potatoes. Hard-boiled eggs, cabbage, and tomatoes may be used as well.

1 pound firm tofu, cut through the thickness into ½-inch-thick slices
2 quarts water
1 pound string beans or Chinese yard-long beans, ends snapped and cut into 1½-inch lengths
3 medium-size carrots, cut into matchstick-size shreds
1 pound smallest-possible red or white potatoes
1 head cauliflower (about 1 pound), broken into florets
¼ cup safflower or corn oil
½ pound bean sprouts, rinsed and drained

TO SERVE:
1 head iceberg lettuce, core trimmed, leaves separated, pressed to flatten, rinsed, drained, and arranged in layers around the rim of a serving platter
Indonesian Peanut-Coconut Dressing (page 156)

1. Wrap the tofu slices in paper towels or a cotton dish towel and place a heavy weight, such as a cast-iron skillet, on top. Let stand for 30 minutes to press out the excess water. Cut into matchstick-size shreds about 2 inches long and ½ inch thick.

2. Bring the water to a boil in a large pot. Separately cook the string beans (about 6 minutes), carrots (6 minutes), potatoes (12 to 14 minutes), and cauliflower (8 to 10 minutes) until just tender, rinsing each vegetable under cold running water once it is cooked and draining thoroughly. Cut the potatoes (with the skin) into slices about ½ inch thick.

3. Heat a wok or a large heavy skillet over high heat until very hot. Add the oil and heat until very hot (about 375 degrees F). Fry the tofu in batches until golden brown, turning several times. Remove with a slotted spoon and drain on paper towels.

4. Arrange the string beans in a layer on top of the lettuce, then arrange the fried tofu, the carrots, potatoes, cauliflower, and bean sprouts in separate concentric circles on top.

5. Pour the warm peanut-coconut dressing over the vegetables. To eat, spoon some of the vegetables and dressing onto a lettuce leaf, roll it up, tucking in the sides, and eat with your fingers.

MAKES 6 SERVINGS

Saucy Vegetable Roll-ups

Too often, vegetarian dishes tend to be bland and somewhat drab. That could never be said for this rainbow-colored salad, spiced generously with garlic, chili paste, and sweet bean paste or hoisin sauce. I like to serve this dish as a light lunch or dinner. To round out the meal, you could serve a soup.

1 pound firm tofu, cut horizontally through the thickness into ½-inch-thick slices

2 small carrots, grated or shredded (about 2 cups)

1 medium-size daikon radish or jicama, peeled, parboiled in water to cover for 5 minutes, and grated or shredded (3 to 4 cups)

3 cups bean sprouts, rinsed and drained

1 medium-size red bell pepper, cored, seeded, and cut into thin julienne strips

1 medium-size yellow bell pepper, cored, seeded, and cut into thin julienne strips

FOR THE SPICY SAUCE:

1 teaspoon safflower or corn oil

1½ tablespoons minced garlic

1 teaspoon hot chili paste, or to taste

7 tablespoons Chinese sweet bean paste or hoisin sauce

1½ tablespoons toasted sesame oil

1½ tablespoons sugar

1 tablespoon soy sauce

3 tablespoons water

TO SERVE:

1½ tablespoons minced scallion greens

2 heads Boston lettuce, cores trimmed, leaves separated, pressed to flatten, rinsed, drained, and arranged in a basket

1. Wrap the tofu slices in paper towels or a cotton dish towel and place a heavy weight, such as a cast-iron skillet, on top. Let stand for 30 minutes to press out the excess water. Cut into matchstick-size shreds about 2 inches long.

2. Arrange the tofu, carrots, daikon or jicama, bean sprouts, and red and yellow pepper strips in mounds or concentric circles in a serving bowl.

3. To prepare the sauce, heat a wok or a large heavy skillet over high heat until very hot. Add the safflower or corn oil and heat until very hot. Add the garlic and chili paste and stir-fry until fragrant, about 10 seconds. Add the remaining sauce ingredients and cook over medium heat until the sauce reduces and becomes thick, about 10 minutes. Spoon into a serving bowl.

4. To serve, pour the spicy sauce over the vegetables, toss lightly, and sprinkle with the minced scallion greens. To eat, spoon a portion of the saucy vegetables onto a lettuce leaf, roll it up, tucking in the sides, and eat with your fingers.

MAKES 6 SERVINGS

Entrée Wraps
and Roll-ups

Grilled Miso Salmon with Sweet-and-Sour Cucumbers ❧ Grilled Ginger Chicken ❧ Vietnamese Shrimp Pancakes ❧ Mu Shu Shrimp ❧ Flash-Cooked Chicken with Leeks ❧ Hot-and-Sour Scallops with Broccoli ❧ Curried Coconut Chicken ❧ Saucy Korean Rolls ❧ Malaysian Pork Rolls ❧ Lion's Head Cabbage Rolls ❧ Lemongrass Beef Wraps ❧ Seared Garlic Beef with Roasted Rainbow Peppers ❧ Grilled Lamb with Flash-Cooked Fennel ❧

When I was a child, mu shu pork was one of the first authentic Asian dishes to penetrate my macaroni-and-cheese bubble. Imagine my delight at receiving two heaping platters of food covered by domed lids, then to lift off the cover of one and inhale the delicious and exotic odor of a freshly cooked mu shu. The garlicky seasonings mingled with the aroma of the seared vegetables.

But the pancakes were what really delighted and intrigued me. They were so thin and delicate, yet so pliable. And the bean sauce that was brushed onto the pancakes was so sticky and rich. It was heaven!

I still take an almost child-like delight in sampling the myriad selections of entrée roll-ups prepared by Asian chefs. I can remember the wonder and enjoyment of discovering Vietnamese grilled meats and seafood: the pleasure of savoring the slightly charred slices of meat complemented by the crunchy vegetables and fresh herbs, all rolled up in a crisp lettuce leaf and dipped in a fiery sweet-and-sour sauce. Ecstasy! Nor will I forget the initial excitement of eating a superb Korean roll-up with ground beef and tender chunks of tofu in a spicy bean sauce. (I make a version with ground turkey that's no less delicious.)

Because so many Asian main dishes lend themselves neatly to the roll-up concept, I have adapted and revised many for this chapter. For instance, the succulent Cantonese classic beef with peppers in black bean sauce is given a contemporary twist by marinating the beef, then grilling, slicing, and tossing it in a garlicky sauce with rainbow peppers. It is served in steamed flour tortillas that have been lightly brushed with toasted sesame oil. Stuffed cabbage is given new meaning with my Lion's Head Cabbage Rolls, for which Napa cabbage leaves are filled with a succulent ground pork mixture seasoned with black mushrooms and fresh ginger. Grilled miso-coated salmon, a dish inspired by a Japanese classic, is complemented by crisp sweet-and-sour cucumber pickles and served in lettuce leaves. And the Malaysian specialty of barbecued pork drenched in a sumptuous oyster sauce is paired here with crisp-cooked green beans and rolled up in pancakes.

With many of the dishes, I have merely substituted wrappers for the more familiar staple of rice. The wrappers may take the more traditional form of Mandarin pancakes (a recipe is included on page 12, but you can cheat and order them from a Chinese restaurant), or use steamed buns (page 14) or fresh spring roll wrappers. They may also be served with good-quality flour tortillas, which work quite nicely if they are steamed and lightly brushed with sesame oil. Other dishes are served wrapped in various lettuces and greens.

The custom of serving stir-fried or cooked food in wrappers originated many years ago in northern China, where wheat replaces rice as the dominant grain. Despite the fact that I have revised and streamlined many of these classic dishes, I know that in my heart my old master chef mentors would heartily approve.

Grilled Miso Salmon with Sweet-and-Sour Cucumbers

I love grilled salmon, because the high heat sears the meat and melts the fat. In this dish, the cooked miso forms a tender crust, sealing in the fish's juices. Complemented by the pickled cucumber, the salmon is truly delicious. I like to serve this dish as a light lunch or dinner.

3 English seedless cucumbers or
   10 Kirby cucumbers, rinsed and
   drained

FOR THE DRESSING, mixed together:
2¼ teaspoons salt
¾ cup Japanese rice vinegar
¾ cup sugar
1 tablespoon peeled and minced fresh
   ginger
1½ pounds salmon fillets, skin on

FOR THE MARINADE, mixed together:
3 tablespoons medium-colored miso
   (*chu miso* or *shinsu ichi miso*),
   or to taste
3 tablespoons mirin (sweetened rice
   wine) or 3 tablespoons sake mixed
   with 1½ tablespoons sugar
1½ teaspoons toasted sesame oil
2 tablespoons minced scallion greens
1 tablespoon peeled and minced fresh
   ginger

TO SERVE:
2 to 3 heads butter or Boston lettuce,
   cores trimmed, leaves separated,
   pressed to flatten, rinsed, drained,
   and arranged in layers around the
   rim of a serving platter
2 tablespoons chopped fresh dill

1. Trim the ends of the cucumbers, slice them lengthwise in half, remove the seeds, and cut crosswise into paper-thin slices. Place in a bowl, add 1½ teaspoons of the salt, and toss lightly. Let sit for 20 minutes.

2. Drain the cucumber, squeeze out the excess water, and return to the bowl. Mix together the rice vinegar, sugar, ginger, and the remaining ¾ teaspoon salt, stirring until the sugar dissolves. Add to the cucumbers, toss lightly, and cover with plastic wrap. Let marinate for 30 minutes, or longer if possible, in the refrigerator, tossing occasionally.

3. Meanwhile, place the salmon in a large bowl. Add the marinade and toss lightly with your hands to coat the salmon. Cover with plastic wrap and refrigerate for 30 minutes or up to several hours, turning several times.

4. Prepare a hot fire for grilling or preheat the oven to 475 degrees F. Place the fillets about 3 inches from the source of heat or on a baking sheet on the upper rack of the oven and grill or bake, brushing with any excess marinade up until the last 5 minutes, until the fish is opaque, 4 to 5 minutes on each side. Remove and cut the fillets into 1-inch sections along the grain of the fish.

5. Arrange the cucumbers in the center of the platter of lettuce. Arrange the salmon fillets on top. Sprinkle with the chopped dill. To eat, spoon some of the salmon with the pickled cucumbers onto a lettuce leaf, roll up, tucking in the edges, and eat with your fingers.

MAKES 6 SERVINGS

Grilled Ginger Chicken

This ginger-teriyaki sauce is simple to prepare and it's delicious with all types of grilled meats and seafood. During grilling season, I often make a large batch, refrigerate it in a tightly sealed container, and use it for several weeks.

FOR THE GINGER-TERIYAKI SAUCE:
¾ cup soy sauce
¾ cup water
⅔ cup rice wine or sake
7 tablespoons sugar
2½ tablespoons peeled and minced
  fresh ginger
1¼ teaspoons crushed red pepper
  (optional)
2½ tablespoons cornstarch

FOR THE GRILL:
1½ pounds skinless, boneless chicken
  breasts, trimmed of fat
2 tablespoons safflower or corn oil
3 medium-size red bell peppers, cored,
  seeded, and cut into ½-inch dice
10 scallions, ends trimmed and cut
  into 1-inch lengths
Twelve 10-inch-long bamboo skewers,
  soaked in water to cover for 1 hour
  and drained

TO SERVE:
2 heads leafy lettuce, cores trimmed,
  leaves separated, pressed to flatten,
  rinsed, drained, and arranged in
  concentric circles in a basket or on
  a serving platter

1. In a medium-size saucepan, combine the sauce ingredients and simmer over medium heat until thickened, stirring constantly to prevent lumps. Remove and let cool for about 10 minutes.

2. Cut the chicken into 1-inch cubes and place in a medium-size bowl. Add one third of the sauce, toss lightly to coat, and let sit refrigerated for 1 hour, or cover with plastic wrap and refrigerate for as long as overnight. Set the remaining ginger sauce aside at room temperature for up to 1 hour, or cover and refrigerate.

3. Prepare a medium-hot fire for grilling. Place the grill rack about 3 inches above the coals. Brush the grill rack generously with oil and heat.

4. Thread the red peppers, chicken, and scallions alternately onto the skewers, starting and ending with the red peppers.

5. Arrange the skewered chicken and vegetables on the grill and grill until the chicken is golden brown and firm to the touch, 10 to 12 minutes, turning once. Baste the chicken and vegetables several times with the ginger sauce up until a few minutes before the meat is cooked. Brush the grill with more oil as needed.

6. Meanwhile, reheat the reserved ginger sauce.

7. Remove the cooked chicken and vegetables from the skewers and arrange on a serving platter. To eat, spoon some of the warm ginger sauce into the center of a lettuce leaf, arrange some of the grilled chicken and vegetables on top, roll up, tucking in the edges, and eat with your fingers.

MAKES 6 SERVINGS

Vietnamese Shrimp Pancakes

I first tasted these superb pancakes filled with fresh vegetables and shrimp several years ago in a little café in Saigon, or Ho Chi Minh City. Traditionally, the pancakes are made with rice powder and coconut milk. I've adapted the recipe and prepare delicate egg crêpes seasoned with turmeric. The dish is light but filling.

1. Pour the dipping sauce into a bowl. Add the grated carrots and let marinate for 20 minutes.

2. Meanwhile, using a sharp knife, slice the shrimp lengthwise in half down the back. Heat the water in a medium-size saucepan until boiling. Add the shrimp and cook until the shrimp are opaque, about 1½ minutes after the water has reached a boil again. Drain in a colander, rinse under cold running water, and drain again.

3. To prepare the pancakes, beat the eggs, water, salt, turmeric together in a medium-size bowl. Using a paper towel dipped in the oil, wipe the inside of a 9- or a 10-inch nonstick frying pan. Heat over medium-high heat until hot (a little water sprinkled should evaporate immediately). Ladle ¼ cup of the egg mixture into the pan and tilt the pan to form a thin circle. Cook briefly until set, about 10 seconds. Flip over, using a spatula, and cook very briefly on the other side. Remove and let cool, stacking the pancakes on a plate as you cook the remaining eggs. There should be 7 to 8 pancakes. Cut the pancakes in half or into quarters and arrange around the outer edge of a serving platter.

4. Drain the carrots. Arrange the shrimp in the center of the serving platter and arrange the carrots, bean sprouts, and scallion greens in concentric circles around the shrimp.

5. Sprinkle the chopped cilantro and basil on top of the shrimp and vegetables. Drizzle the dipping sauce over the shrimp and vegetable mixture and toss lightly; or serve the dipping sauce on the side. To eat, spoon some of the shrimp-veggie mixture into an egg pancake, roll up, and eat with your fingers.

MAKES 6 SERVINGS

1½ recipes Vietnamese Sweet-and-Sour Dipping Sauce (page 152)
2½ cups grated carrots
1 pound medium-size raw shrimp, peeled, deveined, rinsed, drained, and patted dry
4 cups water

FOR THE PANCAKES:
5 large eggs, lightly beaten
2 tablespoons water
1 teaspoon salt
1 teaspoon turmeric
1 teaspoon safflower or corn oil

TO SERVE:
3 cups bean sprouts, rinsed and drained
½ cup scallion greens cut into 1-inch sections
⅓ cup coarsely chopped cilantro (fresh coriander) leaves
⅓ cup coarsely chopped fresh basil leaves

Mu Shu Shrimp

I tasted my first mu shu dish in the sixties. It was prepared by the venerable chefs at Joyce Chen's restaurant in Cambridge, Massachusetts, and I loved it. Mu shu dishes have now established a solid place in the repertoire of Chinese-American restaurant classics. Here's my seafood version of this delicious dish.

1½ pounds medium-size raw shrimp, peeled, deveined, rinsed, drained, and patted dry

FOR THE MARINADE, mixed together:
1½ tablespoons rice wine or sake
1 tablespoon peeled and minced fresh ginger
1 teaspoon toasted sesame oil

FOR THE STIR-FRY:
5 tablespoons canola or corn oil
1 large egg, lightly beaten
3 tablespoons minced garlic
3½ tablespoons peeled and minced fresh ginger
10 dried Chinese black mushrooms, softened in hot water for 20 minutes, drained, stems removed, and caps shredded
4½ cups trimmed, well washed, and finely julienned leeks (the whites and 1 inch of the green parts)
4 cups cored and finely julienned Chinese (Napa) cabbage
2 tablespoons rice wine or sake

FOR THE SAUCE, mixed together:
¼ cup soy sauce
3 tablespoons rice wine or sake
1 teaspoon sugar
⅓ teaspoon freshly ground black pepper
1 teaspoon cornstarch

TO SERVE:
24 Mandarin Pancakes (page 12) or flour tortillas, brushed lightly with toasted sesame oil, folded into quarters, steamed for 10 minutes, arranged on a serving platter or in a basket, and covered with a dish towel to keep warm
¾ cup hoisin sauce, mixed with 1 tablespoon soy sauce and 2½ tablespoons water and placed in a serving dish

1. Cut the shrimp lengthwise in half down the back. Place in a medium-size bowl and add the marinade. Toss lightly to coat, cover with plastic wrap, and refrigerate for 20 minutes.

2. Heat a wok or a large heavy skillet over high heat until very hot. Add 1½ tablespoons of the oil and heat until very hot, about 20 seconds. Drain the shrimp, add to the pan, and stir-fry until they change color, separate, and are opaque, about 2½ minutes. Remove with a handled strainer and drain in a colander. Wipe out the pan.

continued

3. Reheat the pan over high heat until very hot. Add 1 tablespoon of the oil and heat until hot, about 15 seconds. Add the egg and stir-fry to scramble, then move the egg to the side of the pan.

4. Add the remaining 2½ tablespoons oil and heat until very hot. Add the garlic, ginger, and mushrooms, stir to mix, and stir-fry until fragrant, about 10 seconds. Add the leeks and cabbage and toss lightly for 1½ minutes, then add the rice wine and cook until the vegetables are crisp-tender, about 1 minute. Add the sauce. Toss lightly and cook until thickened, stirring constantly to prevent lumps; then add the shrimp, tossing to mix.

5. To eat, place a wrapper on a plate, smear a tablespoon of the hoisin mixture over the wrapper, and spoon some of the stir-fried mixture on top. Roll up and eat with your fingers.

MAKES 6 SERVINGS

Flash-Cooked Chicken with Leeks

In northern China, shredded meats with slivers of scallions are bathed in a rich bean sauce and served in lacy Mandarin pancakes; here I substitute flour tortillas. Pork is the usual meat, but chicken and turkey are also delicious. I like to stir-fry slivers of garlic lightly with leeks or scallions as an edible bed for the tender cooked meat.

1. Lay the chicken breasts on a cutting board. Holding the blade of your knife almost horizontal to the board, cut the chicken crosswise into slices about ⅛ inch thick and 2½ inches long. Place in a bowl, add the marinade, and toss lightly to coat.

2. Heat a wok or a large heavy skillet over high heat until very hot. Add 3½ tablespoons of the oil and heat until very hot, about 30 seconds. Add the chicken slices and stir-fry until the meat becomes opaque and is cooked through, about 2 minutes. Drain in a colander.

3. Reheat the pan over high heat until very hot. Add the remaining 2 tablespoons oil and heat until very hot. Add the garlic and leeks and stir-fry, tossing, for about 1 minute. Add the rice wine and cook until the leeks are tender, about 1 minute. Spoon onto a serving platter. Wipe out the pan.

4. Reheat the pan over high heat until hot. Add the sauce and heat until boiling, then add the cooked chicken and toss lightly to coat evenly with the sauce.

5. Scoop up the chicken mixture and arrange over the leeks and garlic on the platter. To eat, spoon some of the stir-fried chicken and leeks onto a tortilla, roll up, and eat with your fingers.

MAKES 6 SERVINGS

1½ pounds skinless, boneless chicken breasts, trimmed of fat

FOR THE MARINADE, mixed together:
3 tablespoons soy sauce
1½ tablespoons peeled and minced fresh ginger
1 teaspoon toasted sesame oil
2 teaspoons cornstarch

FOR THE STIR-FRY:
5½ tablespoons safflower or corn oil
10 cloves garlic, very thinly sliced
6 cups shredded and well washed leeks (about 3; the whites and 1 inch of the green parts)
2 tablespoons rice wine or sake

FOR THE SAUCE, mixed together:
5 tablespoons sweet bean or hoisin sauce
3½ tablespoons sugar
3 tablespoons water
1 tablespoon soy sauce

TO SERVE:
18 flour tortillas, brushed lightly with toasted sesame oil, folded into quarters, steamed for 10 minutes, arranged in a basket or serving bowl, and covered with a dish towel to keep warm

Hot-and-Sour Scallops with Broccoli

Sweet scallops and broccoli drenched in a pungent chili-garlic-black-vinegar sauce are superb wrapped in crisp romaine lettuce leaves. I make numerous variations on this recipe, substituting chicken or other types of seafood for the scallops, and snow or snap peas for the broccoli.

1½ pounds sea scallops, rinsed,
    drained, patted dry, and sliced
    horizontally in half if very thick

FOR THE MARINADE, mixed together:
3 tablespoons rice wine or sake
1½ tablespoons peeled and
    minced fresh ginger
1 teaspoon toasted sesame oil

TO FINISH:
3 quarts water
1 head Chinese (Napa) cabbage,
    leaves separated and stems
    trimmed

1 pound broccoli, stalks trimmed
    and peeled, florets separated,
    and stalks cut into 1-inch
    lengths
1½ tablespoons safflower or corn
    oil
1 heaping teaspoon hot chili paste
2½ tablespoons minced garlic
1 medium-size red onion, cut into
    thin julienne strips

FOR THE HOT-AND-SOUR SAUCE,
    mixed together:
1 cup Basic Chinese Chicken
    Broth (page 17) or water
3½ tablespoons soy sauce
2½ tablespoons rice wine or sake
1½ tablespoons sugar
1 tablespoon Chinese black
    vinegar or Worcestershire sauce
1 teaspoon toasted sesame oil
1½ tablespoons cornstarch

1. In a medium-size bowl, mix together the scallops and marinade, tossing lightly to coat. Set aside.

2. Bring the water to a boil in a large pot. Add the cabbage leaves and blanch for 4 seconds. Remove and refresh under cold running water. Drain and arrange around the edges of a serving platter.

3. Reheat the water to boiling. Add the broccoli. Cook until just tender, about 4 minutes for the stems and 3 minutes for the florets. Remove and refresh under cold running water. Drain thoroughly.

4. Reheat the water to boiling, add the scallops, and cook just until slightly undercooked, about 1½ minutes. Remove with a handled strainer and drain well.

5. Heat a wok or a large heavy skillet over high heat. Add the oil and heat, about 20 seconds. Add the chili paste, garlic, and red onion and stir-fry over medium-high heat until the onion starts to soften, 1½ to 2 minutes. Add the sauce mixture and cook, stirring to prevent lumps, until thickened. Add the scallops and mix carefully.

6. Transfer the scallop mixture to the serving platter. To eat, spoon some of the scallop mixture into a cabbage leaf, fold it over, roll up, tucking in the edges, and eat with your fingers.

MAKES 6 SERVINGS

Curried Coconut Chicken

The fragrant curry seasoning in this dish is a wonderful blending of fresh lemongrass, chili peppers, cumin, coriander, and fresh ginger. I often steam extra pancakes, since my family and friends hate to leave any sauce behind and like to wipe the platter clean.

1½ pounds skinless, boneless chicken breasts, trimmed of fat

FOR THE MARINADE:
1½ tablespoons soy sauce
1½ tablespoons rice wine or sake

FOR THE STIR-FRY:
5½ tablespoons safflower or corn oil
2 medium-size red onions, cut into julienne strips

FOR THE CURRY SEASONINGS, finely chopped together in a food processor or a blender:
3 dried red chili peppers or 1½ teaspoons crushed red pepper

2 stalks fresh lemongrass, outer leaves removed, ends trimmed, and stalks cut into 2-inch sections
Two ½-inch-thick slices peeled fresh ginger
1½ teaspoons ground cumin
1½ teaspoons ground coriander
½ teaspoon freshly ground black pepper
1 teaspoon salt

FOR THE SAUCE, mixed together:
1¼ cups unsweetened coconut milk (mix well before using)
3 tablespoons fish sauce
1 tablespoon sugar

TO FINISH:
1½ cups frozen peas, defrosted
1 cup packed fresh basil leaves, rinsed, drained, and coarsely chopped

TO SERVE:
18 flour tortillas, brushed lightly with toasted sesame oil, folded into quarters, steamed for 10 minutes, arranged on a serving platter or in a basket, and covered with a dish towel to keep warm

1. Cut the chicken breasts lengthwise in half, then, holding the knife at a 45-degree angle to the cutting board, cut crosswise into thin slices about 1 inch long and ⅛ inch thick. Place the slices in a medium-size bowl, add the marinade ingredients, toss lightly, and refrigerate for 20 minutes, or as long as overnight.

2. Heat a wok or a large heavy skillet over high heat until very hot. Add 3½ tablespoons of the oil and heat until very hot, about 20 seconds. Add the chicken and stir-fry until the meat becomes opaque and the slices separate. Remove with a handled strainer and drain in a colander. Wipe out the pan.

3. Reheat the pan over high heat until very hot, then add the remaining 2 tablespoons oil and heat for 20 seconds over medium-low heat. Add the onions and curry seasonings and cook, stirring, until the onions are tender, 3 to 4 minutes. Add the sauce and cook until the sauce has thickened slightly. Return the chicken to the pan, increase the heat to medium-high, add the peas and basil, and toss lightly together.

4. Spoon the mixture onto a serving platter. To eat, spoon some of the chicken mixture onto a tortilla, roll up, and eat with your fingers.

MAKES 6 SERVINGS

Saucy Korean Rolls

I was first introduced to this dish in a delightful Korean restaurant in Los Angeles's Koreatown. The contrasting crisp-tender textures and spicy-saucy flavors made it memorable. Traditionally it is prepared with beef, but I like to substitute lean ground turkey for a healthful alternative.

½ pound firm tofu, cut into 1-inch-thick slices
1 pound lean ground turkey

FOR THE MEAT SEASONINGS, mixed together:
2 tablespoons soy sauce
1½ tablespoons peeled and minced fresh ginger
½ tablespoon toasted sesame oil

FOR THE STIR-FRY:
2 tablespoons safflower or corn oil
3½ tablespoons minced scallion whites
1½ tablespoons minced garlic
1 teaspoon hot chili paste, or to taste
1½ cups canned whole water chestnuts, blanched in boiling water for 10 seconds, refreshed under cold running water, drained, blotted dry, and coarsely chopped

FOR THE SPICY SAUCE, mixed together:
7 tablespoons Chinese sweet bean paste or hoisin sauce
¼ cup sugar
3 tablespoons water

TO SERVE:
1½ tablespoons minced scallion greens
2 heads Boston lettuce, cores trimmed, leaves separated, pressed to flatten, rinsed, drained, and arranged in a basket

1. Wrap the tofu in paper towels or a cotton dish towel and place a heavy weight, such as a cast-iron skillet, on top. Let stand for 30 minutes to press out excess water, then cut into ¼-inch dice.

2. In a medium-size bowl, mix together the turkey and meat seasonings.

3. Heat a wok or large heavy skillet over high heat for 15 seconds. Add ½ tablespoon of the oil and heat until hot, about 30 seconds. Add the turkey and stir-fry over medium-high heat, mashing to break up any clumps, until the meat changes color and separates. Drain in a colander and wipe out the pan.

4. Reheat the pan, add the remaining 1½ tablespoons oil, and heat over high heat until very hot. Add the scallion whites, garlic, and chili paste and stir-fry until fragrant, about 15 seconds. Add the water chestnuts and toss lightly until heated through. Add the spicy sauce mixture and cook, stirring, until thickened. Add the tofu dice and cooked turkey and toss to coat with the sauce. Cover and cook for about 1½ minutes to heat through.

5. Spoon the stir-fry onto a serving platter and sprinkle the minced scallion greens on top. To eat, spoon some of the stir-fried mixture onto a lettuce leaf, roll it up, tucking in the edges, and eat with your fingers.

MAKES 6 SERVINGS

Malaysian Pork Rolls

Succulent, tender roasted pork marinated in a heady Malaysian marinade and tossed with crisp green beans in a spicy oyster sauce is a meal in itself when wrapped in tender flour tortillas.

1½ pounds sirloin or center-cut pork fillets or tenderloin or center-cut boneless chops, trimmed of fat and gristle

FOR THE ROASTING SAUCE:
4½ tablespoons oyster sauce
2 tablespoons soy sauce
1½ tablespoons ketchup
1½ tablespoons packed light brown sugar
2 tablespoons minced garlic
1½ tablespoons peeled and minced fresh ginger
5 small shallots, minced
1½ teaspoons hot chili paste

FOR THE STIR-FRY:
1½ teaspoons corn or safflower oil
1½ tablespoons peeled and minced fresh ginger
1 teaspoon hot chili paste
2 cups scallion greens cut into ½-inch sections
1½ pounds green beans, ends trimmed and cut into 2-inch lengths

FOR THE STIR-FRY SAUCE, mixed together:
1 cup Basic Chinese Chicken Broth (page 17) or water
4½ tablespoons oyster sauce
2½ tablespoons rice wine or sake

1½ teaspoons soy sauce
2 teaspoons cornstarch

TO SERVE:
18 flour tortillas, brushed lightly with toasted sesame oil, folded into quarters, steamed for 10 minutes, arranged in a basket or bowl, and covered with a dish towel to keep warm

1. Put the pork in a bowl. Add the roasting sauce and rub it all over the pork. Cover with plastic wrap and let marinate in the refrigerator for at least 2 hours, or overnight, if possible.

2. Preheat the oven to 425 degrees F.

3. Place the pork, with the marinade, in a roasting pan or on a cookie sheet that has been lined with aluminum foil. Roast until the internal temperature registers about 160 degrees F on a meat thermometer, about 45 minutes. Remove from the oven and let cool slightly. Cut the meat across the grain into thin slices about ¼ inch thick and 1½ inches long.

4. Heat a wok or a large heavy skillet over high heat until very hot. Add the oil and heat until very hot, about 20 seconds. Add the ginger, chili paste, and scallions and stir-fry until fragrant, about 15 seconds. Add the green beans and stir-fry for about a minute, then add the stir-fry sauce mixture. Cover, reduce the heat to low, and cook until the beans are just tender, about 4 minutes. Uncover, increase the heat to high, and cook until the sauce is thickened, stirring to prevent lumps. Add the pork and toss lightly to mix. Spoon onto a serving platter. To eat, spoon some of the pork mixture onto a tortilla, roll up, and eat with your fingers.

MAKES 6 SERVINGS

Lion's Head Cabbage Rolls

I have been a huge fan of stuffed cabbage ever since the day I first tasted my great-aunt Sophie's mouthwatering version. Years later, I developed a passion for Lion's Head, a sumptuous Chinese stew made with Napa cabbage and ground meat. Here's my adapted "stuffed cabbage rolls" variation, a cross between the Jewish and Chinese dishes. It tastes even better when reheated.

1 large head Chinese (Napa) cabbage (2½ to 3 pounds), outer leaves discarded

3 quarts water

FOR THE FILLING:

1 pound lean ground pork

10 dried Chinese black mushrooms, softened in hot water, drained, stems removed, and large caps cut in half

2½ tablespoons peeled and minced fresh ginger

2 tablespoons minced scallion whites

2 tablespoons soy sauce

1 teaspoon toasted sesame oil

2 tablespoons cornstarch

TO COOK THE CABBAGE ROLLS:

1 teaspoon safflower or corn oil

6 cloves garlic, smashed lightly with the flat side of a knife

¼ cup rice wine or sake

4½ cups Basic Chinese Chicken Broth (page 17)

1 teaspoon salt, or to taste

Soy sauce to taste (optional)

1. Separate the cabbage into individual leaves, rinse, and drain. Using a sharp knife, make a small V in the bottom of 17 or 18 leaves and cut away the stem section. Bring the water to a boil in a large pot. Drop the cabbage leaves into the water and boil for 1 minute. Remove with a handled strainer and refresh under cold running water. Drain on paper towels. Cut the remaining cabbage leaves into 2-inch squares, separating the stem sections from the leafy ones.

2. In a large bowl, combine the filling ingredients, tossing the mixture to combine it well; it will be very fragrant and sticky. Shape 2 tablespoons of the filling into a cylinder about 2 inches long. Place the meat in the center of a cabbage leaf and roll it up, folding in the sides to completely enclose the filling. Repeat with the remaining filling and cabbage leaves.

3. Heat a large casserole or large pot over medium-high heat until very hot. Add the oil and heat until hot, about 10 seconds. Add the garlic and cabbage squares and stir-fry over high heat for 10 seconds, then add the rice wine, broth, and salt. Heat until boiling, then reduce the heat to medium and cook for 20 minutes.

4. Using a spatula, move the cooked cabbage aside and add the cabbage rolls, seam side down, to the pot, arranging them neatly. Partially cover the pot and bring the liquid to a boil again. Reduce the heat to medium and cook for 45 minutes, skimming the surface of the liquid several times to remove any impurities. Taste the broth for seasoning, adding soy sauce or salt if necessary. Serve the cabbage rolls with the broth from the pot.

MAKES 6 SERVINGS

Lemongrass Beef Wraps

One of the most classic Vietnamese dishes is slices of beef individually seared over a hot grill at the table and wrapped with vegetables in lettuce leaves. I make a slightly easier version by first marinating the meat in flavorful seasonings, grilling it over a hot fire, and slicing it, then tossing the cooked slices with red onions in a light sauce. The mixture is then easily scooped up by the spoonful and wrapped in fresh lettuce leaves. The spicy dressing adds a last touch, to make the dish unforgettable.

1½ pounds flank steak or London broil, trimmed of fat and gristle

FOR THE MARINADE, ground to a paste in a blender or a food processor:

2 stalks fresh lemongrass, outer leaves removed, ends trimmed, and stalks cut into 1-inch sections
4 cloves garlic, peeled
1 teaspoon crushed red pepper, or to taste
3 tablespoons fish sauce

¼ teaspoon freshly ground black pepper
1½ teaspoons cornstarch

FOR THE GRILL AND STIR-FRY:

2½ tablespoons safflower or corn oil
2 medium-size red onions, cut into thin julienne strips
1½ tablespoons rice wine

FOR THE SAUCE, mixed together:

1½ tablespoons fish sauce
1 tablespoon sugar

TO SERVE:

1 cup cilantro (fresh coriander) leaves, roughly chopped
3 tablespoons chopped dry-roasted peanuts
2 heads Boston lettuce, cores trimmed, leaves separated, pressed to flatten, rinsed, drained, and arranged in a basket or bowl
Vietnamese Sweet-and-Sour Dipping Sauce (page 152)

1. Put the beef in a large bowl. Add the marinade and toss lightly to coat. Cover with plastic wrap and let marinate for 30 minutes at room temperature, or refrigerate for as long as overnight.

2. Prepare a medium-hot fire for grilling. Place the grill rack about 3 inches above the coals. Brush the grill rack generously with 1 tablespoon of the oil and heat. Place the meat on the grill and grill, turning once, about 6 minutes on each side. Baste the beef as it cooks. Let the meat cool and cut across the grain into slices ⅙ inch thick and 3 inches long.

3. Heat a wok or large heavy skillet over high heat until hot. Add the remaining 1½ tablespoons oil and heat until very hot. Add the red onions and stir-fry for about 30 seconds over medium heat, then add the rice wine and continue cooking until the onions soften, about a minute. Add the cooked beef, the sauce, and toss lightly over high heat to coat.

4. Put the beef and onions in a serving dish. Sprinkle with the cilantro and peanuts. To eat, spoon some beef onto a lettuce leaf, roll up, tucking in the edges, dip in the sweet-and-sour sauce, and eat with your fingers.

MAKES 6 SERVINGS

Seared Garlic Beef with Roasted Rainbow Peppers

I like to think of these rolls as Chinese fajitas, but (dare I say it?) they're even better. Marinated grilled slices of beef are stir-fried with rainbow peppers and snow peas, then bathed in a garlicky black bean sauce and served in soft flour tortillas.

1½ pounds flank steak or London
    broil, trimmed of fat and gristle

FOR THE MARINADE:
2 tablespoons minced garlic
3 tablespoons soy sauce
1½ teaspoons toasted sesame oil

FOR THE GRILL:
2 tablespoons safflower or corn oil

FOR THE STIR-FRY:
2 tablespoons safflower or corn oil
2 tablespoons fermented or salted
    black beans, rinsed, drained,
    and minced
2 tablespoons minced garlic

1½ tablespoons peeled and
    minced fresh ginger
1 medium-size red onion, cut into
    very thin julienne strips
1 medium-size red bell pepper,
    cored, seeded, and cut into
    thin julienne strips
1 medium-size yellow bell pepper,
    cored, seeded, and cut into
    thin julienne strips
1 medium-size orange bell pepper,
    cored, seeded, and cut into
    thin julienne strips

FOR THE SAUCE, mixed together:
1 cup Basic Chinese Chicken
    Broth (page 17) or water

5 tablespoons soy sauce
¼ cup rice wine or sake
1½ tablespoons sugar
1½ teaspoons cornstarch

½ pound snow peas, ends
    trimmed and veiny strings
    removed

TO SERVE:
18 flour tortillas, brushed lightly
    with toasted sesame oil, folded
    into quarters, steamed for 10
    minutes, arranged in a basket
    or bowl, and covered with a
    dish towel to keep warm

1. Place the meat in a large bowl, add the marinade, and toss. Marinate for at least 2 hours in the refrigerator.

2. Prepare a medium-hot fire for grilling or preheat the broiler. Place the grill rack 3 inches from the heat source or place the broiler pan on the upper tray. Brush the grill rack with the oil. Grill or broil the beef until medium-rare, about 6 minutes on each side, basting with the marinade once or twice. Let cool slightly, then cut the meat across the grain into thin slices.

3. Heat a wok or a large heavy skillet until very hot. Add the oil and heat until very hot. Add the black beans, garlic, and ginger and stir-fry over medium-high heat, until fragrant, about 15 seconds. Add the red onion and peppers and cook until slightly soft, about 2 minutes. Add the sauce mixture and heat until boiling. Add the snow peas and stir until the sauce is thickened. Add the beef and toss lightly in the sauce.

4. Transfer the beef mixture to a serving platter. To eat, spoon some of the meat and vegetables onto a tortilla, roll up, and eat with your fingers.

MAKES 6 SERVINGS

Grilled Lamb with Flash-Cooked Fennel

I've always adored grilled lamb, seared on the outside and pink within. Cut into thin slices and tossed with slices of fennel, red bell pepper, and scallions in a light dressing, it is superb served in flour tortillas or Mandarin pancakes (page 12). It's a delicious meal-in-itself.

1½ pounds boneless leg of lamb (shank portion) or precut lamb for kebabs, fat and gristle removed

FOR THE MARINADE, mixed together:
¼ cup soy sauce
2 tablespoons sugar
2½ tablespoons minced garlic
1 tablespoon crushed red pepper
1 teaspoon toasted sesame oil

Twelve 10-inch-long bamboo skewers, soaked in cold water for 1 hour and drained
1½ pounds fennel bulbs, rinsed and stalks trimmed

FOR THE STIR-FRY:
2 tablespoons safflower or corn oil
2 tablespoons peeled and finely minced fresh ginger
1 large red or yellow bell pepper, cored, seeded, and cut into thin julienne strips
2 tablespoons rice wine or sake
8 scallions, green part only, cut into 1-inch sections (about 1½ cups)

FOR THE DRESSING, mixed together:
¼ cup soy sauce
2½ tablespoons Chinese black vinegar or Worcestershire sauce
1½ tablespoons sugar

TO SERVE:
18 flour tortillas, brushed lightly with toasted sesame oil, folded into quarters, steamed for 10 minutes, arranged in a basket or serving bowl, and covered with a dish towel to keep warm

1. Cut the lamb into cubes about 1 inch square. Place the pieces in a large bowl. Add the marinade and toss lightly to coat. Let marinate for at least 1 hour at room temperature or as long as overnight in the refrigerator.

2. Thread the lamb onto the bamboo skewers; reserve the marinade.

3. Cut each fennel bulb lengthwise in half, then cut the fennel into thin julienne strips about 2 inches long. Heat a large pot of water until boiling. Add the fennel strips, and cook until crisp-tender, about 2 minutes. Drain in a colander, refresh under cold running water, and drain thoroughly.

4. Prepare a medium-hot fire for grilling or preheat the broiler. Arrange the skewered meat about 3 inches from the heat source and cook until medium-rare, about 4 minutes on each side, turning once and basting with the marinade once or twice. Transfer to a platter and let cool for several minutes, then cut across the grain into thin slices.

continued

5. Heat a wok or large heavy skillet over high heat until very hot. Add the oil and heat until hot. Add the ginger and bell pepper and toss lightly for about 30 seconds, then add the rice wine and stir-fry for another minute. Add the fennel and scallion greens and stir-fry for a minute. Add the lamb slices and dressing and toss to coat the meat and vegetables.

6. Transfer the mixture to a serving platter. To eat, spoon some of the meat and vegetable mixture onto a tortilla, roll up, and eat with your fingers.

MAKES 6 SERVINGS

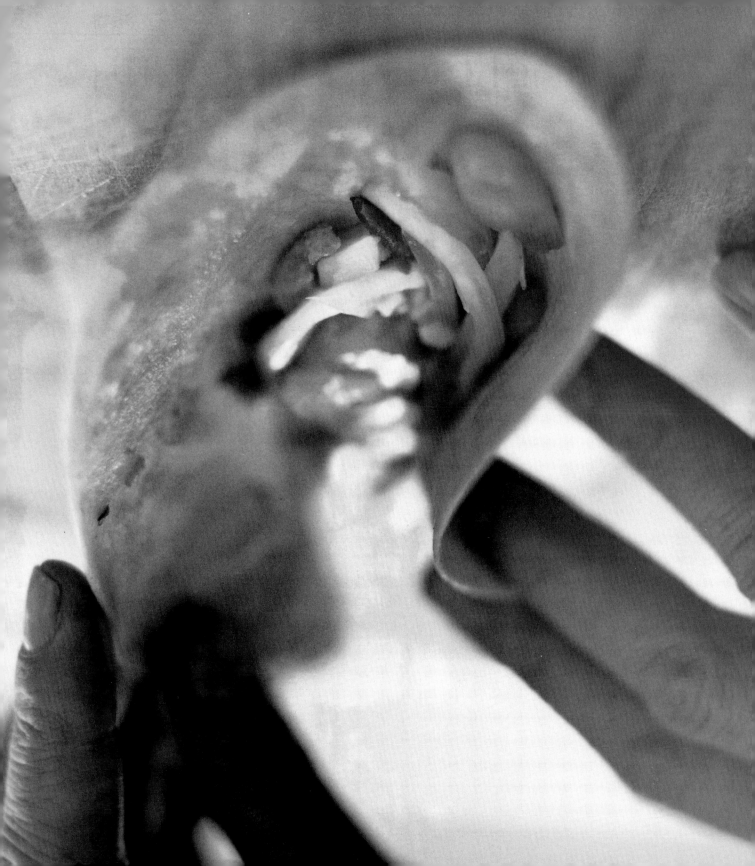

New Asian **Wraps**

CHINESE JERK CHICKEN WITH MANGO SALSA ❧ TANDOORI CHICKEN WITH MANGO CHUTNEY ❧ BARBECUED PORK LOIN WITH ASIAN SLAW ❧ SEARED STEAK WITH WILD MUSHROOMS ❧ GRILLED SHRIMP WITH FRESH SALSA ❧ BARBECUED HALIBUT WITH SPICY CILANTRO PESTO ❧ GRILLED SWORDFISH KEBABS WITH PINEAPPLE SALSA ❧

Some of my favorite new dishes are created by mixing and matching native and Asian ingredients with Western and Eastern cooking techniques. This chapter is a celebration of such dishes.

Imagine slow-grilled, juicy chicken legs that have been marinated in "jerk" seasonings like fresh ginger, mustard powder, basil, and orange juice, served with a tart fresh mango salsa and wrapped in a steamed flour tortilla. ("Jerk" is a tradition of slow-roasting marinated meat that originated in Jamaica.) Or rolls stuffed with slices of garlicky barbecued pork loin topped with ribbons of sweet-and-sour carrot and a freshly prepared cabbage slaw. Try swordfish kebabs paired with pineapple salsa and wrapped in crisp lettuce leaves, or juicy, charcoal-grilled steak smothered with sautéed wild mushrooms.

I call these dishes "New Asian," disdaining the much-maligned term *fusion*. While these recipes may borrow ideas from several cultures, they remain true to the spirit of one classic cuisine, and I feel such dishes are best pared back, made with just a few ingredients rather than embellished with an overabundance.

Many of the dishes in this chapter involve grilling, which is a popular technique in Asia as well as the West. I like to first marinate or season meats and seafood with pungent spice rubs, which highlight their delicious flavor. The hot, freshly grilled foods are superb served with the cool pickles, salsas, chutneys, and slaws. Wrapped in soft flour tortillas or pancakes, they make filling and delicious meals-in-themselves, ideal for any season.

Chinese Jerk Chicken with Mango Salsa

Traditionally, jerk chicken is a slow-cooked delicacy that may take up to an hour over a slow fire. I prepare a streamlined version, cooking chicken quickly over a hot fire. It's not quite as smoky as the original, but it's just as delicious.

FOR THE JERK CHICKEN PASTE, blended to a paste in a blender or a food processor:

6 to 7 small fresh red chili peppers, to your taste, ends trimmed and seeds removed

3½ tablespoons minced scallion whites

2 tablespoons peeled and minced fresh ginger

1½ tablespoons dried basil

2 tablespoons mustard powder

1½ tablespoons ground coriander

1 teaspoon salt

½ teaspoon freshly ground black pepper

¼ cup orange juice

2 tablespoons Japanese rice vinegar

6 boneless chicken legs and thighs, trimmed of excess skin and fat

TO SERVE:

4 cups shredded romaine lettuce leaves, arranged around the rim of a serving platter

18 flour tortillas, brushed lightly with toasted sesame oil, folded into quarters, steamed for 10 minutes, arranged in a basket or serving bowl, and covered with a dish towel to keep warm

Mango Salsa (page 146)

1. Put the jerk paste in a small bowl, cover with plastic wrap, and let sit for 1 hour at room temperature or overnight in the refrigerator.

2. Put the chicken in a large bowl, add the paste, and toss to coat evenly, rubbing the paste into the skin. Cover with plastic wrap and refrigerate for 1 hour.

3. Prepare a hot fire for grilling. Oil the grill rack and place it about 3 inches above the coals. Arrange the chicken on the grill rack and cook, covered, until completely cooked through, 8 to 12 minutes, turning once. Remove and let cool slightly.

4. Cut the chicken into thin slices and arrange in the middle of the platter of lettuce. To eat, put some chicken slices in the middle of a warm tortilla, add some shredded lettuce, spoon some of the salsa on top, roll up the tortilla, and eat with your fingers.

MAKES 6 SERVINGS

Tandoori Chicken with Mango Chutney

My version of tandoori chicken is redolent of garlic, oregano, cumin, hot peppers, and turmeric. Charcoal-grilled and sliced, the chicken is superb paired with a tart mango chutney and wrapped in lettuce and flour tortillas.

1½ pounds boneless, skinless chicken breasts, trimmed of fat

FOR THE TANDOORI MARINADE, mixed together:

1½ cups plain low-fat yogurt
2 tablespoons peeled and minced fresh ginger
1½ tablespoons minced garlic
1 teaspoon crushed red pepper, or to taste
1¼ teaspoons ground cumin
1¼ teaspoons dried oregano
¾ teaspoon turmeric
1 teaspoon salt
½ teaspoon freshly ground black pepper

TO SERVE:

1 medium-size head romaine lettuce, core trimmed, leaves separated, pressed to flatten, rinsed, drained, and arranged in a basket
18 flour tortillas, brushed lightly with toasted sesame oil, folded into quarters, steamed for 10 minutes, arranged in a basket or serving bowl, and covered with a dish towel to keep warm
Mango Chutney (page 158)

1. Put the chicken breasts in a bowl. Lightly prick the meat all over with a fork so that the seasonings can penetrate.

2. Add the marinade to the chicken and toss lightly to coat. Cover with plastic wrap and let marinate in the refrigerator for at least several hours, or overnight if possible.

3. Prepare a hot fire for grilling or heat a large nonstick skillet over high heat until very hot. Oil the grill rack and place it 3 inches above the coals, arrange the chicken on the rack, cover, and grill until cooked through, 8 to 9 minutes per side. Or, sear the chicken in the pan and cook until crispy brown and cooked through, 8 to 12 minutes per side, turning once. Remove, let cool slightly, and cut crosswise into thin slices.

4. To eat, place a lettuce leaf on a tortilla, spoon some slices of chicken on top, add some mango chutney, roll up, and eat with your fingers.

MAKES 6 SERVINGS

Barbecued Pork Loin with Asian Slaw

Both Asian and Caribbean cooks appreciate the splendid flavors of barbecued pork accompanied by vegetable slaws. This is my version of that brilliant pairing.

1½ pounds sirloin or center-cut pork fillets, trimmed of fat and gristle

FOR THE MARINADE, mixed together:
½ cup hoisin sauce
3 tablespoons soy sauce
2½ tablespoons ketchup
1½ tablespoons minced garlic

TO SERVE:
18 flour tortillas, brushed lightly with toasted sesame oil, folded into quarters, steamed for 10 minutes, arranged in a basket or serving bowl, and covered with a dish towel to keep warm
Asian Slaw (page 159)

1. In a large bowl, mix together the pork and marinade, tossing to coat. Cover with plastic wrap and let marinate in the refrigerator for 2 hours.

2. Preheat the oven to 350 degrees F or prepare a hot fire for grilling.

3. If baking the pork, arrange the meat in a pan lined with aluminum foil and roast until cooked through, 30 to 45 minutes. If grilling, place the grill rack 3 inches above the coals, arrange the meat on the rack, and grill until cooked through, 7 to 8 minutes per side (add 1 more minute per side for thicker cuts). Let the pork cool slightly.

4. Cut the pork across the grain into thin slices, about ⅙ inch thick and 3 inches long, and arrange on a serving platter. To eat, put some of the pork slices in the center of a tortilla, spoon some of the cabbage slaw on top, roll up, and eat with your fingers.

MAKES 6 SERVINGS

Seared Steak with Wild Mushrooms

This wrap was inspired by my late mother, who would treat herself (not often enough) to a grilled steak smothered with mushrooms and garlic when my father was traveling and dealing with four small children became too overwhelming.

1½ pounds boneless sirloin, flank steak, or London broil, trimmed of fat or gristle

FOR THE MARINADE, mixed together:
2 tablespoons minced garlic
3 tablespoons soy sauce
1½ teaspoons toasted sesame oil

FOR THE GRILL:
1 tablespoon safflower or corn oil

FOR THE MUSHROOMS:
1 tablespoon safflower or corn oil
12 cloves garlic, smashed with the flat side of a knife and very thinly sliced
½ pound fresh shiitake mushrooms, wiped clean, stems removed, and caps thinly sliced
½ pound fresh maitake mushrooms (sold in supermarkets and otherwise known as "hen of the woods"), rinsed lightly, drained, stem ends trimmed, and thinly sliced

⅓ pound fresh oyster mushrooms, rinsed lightly, drained, stem ends trimmed, and thinly sliced
3½ tablespoons rice wine or sake
3½ tablespoons soy sauce
1½ cups minced scallion greens

TO SERVE:
18 flour tortillas, brushed lightly with toasted sesame oil, folded into quarters, steamed for 10 minutes, arranged in a basket or serving bowl, and covered with a dish towel to keep warm

1. Place the meat in a large bowl, add the marinade, and toss lightly to coat. Cover with plastic wrap and let sit for at least 2 hours or overnight in the refrigerator.

2. Prepare a medium-hot fire for grilling or preheat the broiler. Place the grill rack or broiler pan 3 inches away from the heat source. Brush the grill with the oil. (Alternatively, you can heat a large heavy skillet over high heat, add a teaspoon of oil, and heat until near smoking.) Grill or broil the beef until medium-rare, 7 to 8 minutes on each side, basting once or twice with the marinade (or pan-sear 8 to 12 minutes per side). Let cool slightly and cut the meat across the grain into thin slices.

3. Heat a wok or a large heavy skillet over high heat until very hot. Add the oil and heat until hot, about 20 seconds. Add the garlic and mushrooms and stir-fry briefly. Reduce the heat slightly and add the rice wine. Partially cover and cook until the mushrooms are tender, about 3½ minutes. Uncover and cook to reduce the liquid slightly. Add the soy sauce and scallion greens and mix thoroughly. Scoop the mixture into a serving dish.

4. To eat, arrange some of the meat slices on a tortilla, spoon some of the mushroom mixture on top, roll up, and eat with your fingers.

MAKES 6 SERVINGS

Grilled Shrimp with Fresh Salsa

I will never forget my first taste of grilled shrimp garnished with a fresh tomato-cilantro salsa and wrapped in a steamed flour tortilla on a beach in Mexico. It was so delicious! I started making the dish myself, adding a rice wine–toasted sesame oil marinade. The seasoning is subtle, but it really adds to the flavor of the finished dish.

1½ pounds large raw shrimp, peeled, deveined, rinsed, drained, and patted dry

FOR THE MARINADE:

6 cloves garlic, smashed with the flat side of a knife

3 small hot red Thai peppers, ends trimmed, seeds removed, and thinly sliced (if unavailable, substitute dried *péquin* or hot red Thai peppers, softened in hot water for 15 minutes and drained)

¼ cup rice wine or sake

1½ teaspoons toasted sesame oil

Six 10-inch-long bamboo skewers, soaked in water to cover for 1 hour and drained

TO SERVE:

18 flour tortillas, brushed lightly with toasted sesame oil, folded into quarters, steamed for 10 minutes, arranged in a basket or a serving bowl, and covered with a dish towel to keep warm

Spicy Salsa (page 143)

1. Using a sharp knife, score the shrimp down the back so that they will butterfly when cooked. Place in a bowl or a dish.

2. Add the marinade ingredients to the shrimp, toss lightly, cover with plastic wrap, and let marinate for at least 3 hours or overnight in the refrigerator.

3. Thread the shrimp onto the skewers so that they lie flat.

4. Prepare a medium-hot fire for grilling and place the grill rack about 3 inches above the coals. Arrange the shrimp on the grill and cook until cooked through, 5 to 7 minutes on each side, basting a few times with the marinade up until the last few minutes. Remove the cooked shrimp from the skewers and arrange on a serving platter.

5. To eat, place a grilled shrimp on a warm tortilla, spoon some spicy salsa on top, roll up, and eat with your fingers.

MAKES 6 SERVINGS

Barbecued Halibut with Spicy Cilantro Pesto

Halibut, with its delicate meat, is one of my favorite fish, but you could easily substitute any firm-fleshed fish, such as red snapper or sea bass. This unusual dish brings together sweet, tender seafood, fresh herbs, and crisp grated zucchini to create an unforgettable taste experience.

4 medium-size zucchini (about 1½ pounds), ends trimmed and grated
1 teaspoon salt
1½ pounds halibut steaks, about 1 inch thick, rinsed and drained

FOR THE MARINADE, mixed together:
¼ cup rice wine or sake
1 tablespoon peeled and minced fresh ginger
1 tablespoon minced scallion whites
½ teaspoon salt
2 teaspoons toasted sesame oil

FOR THE SPICY CILANTRO PESTO, blended to a paste in a food processor or a blender:
3 cloves garlic, peeled
½ teaspoon crushed red pepper
1 cup cilantro (fresh coriander) leaves, stems trimmed, rinsed, and drained
½ cup fresh basil leaves, stems trimmed, rinsed, and drained
3 tablespoons toasted sesame oil
1 teaspoon salt

FOR THE DRESSING, mixed together:
½ cup plus 1 tablespoon soy sauce
6 tablespoons Japanese rice vinegar
3 tablespoons sugar
2 tablespoons sweetened rice wine (mirin) or sake

TO SERVE:
18 flour tortillas, brushed lightly with toasted sesame oil, folded into quarters, steamed for 10 minutes, arranged in a basket or a serving bowl, and covered with a dish towel to keep warm

1. Put the grated zucchini in a medium-size bowl, add the salt, toss lightly, and let sit for 1 hour.

2. Put the fish in a bowl. Add the marinade and toss lightly to coat. Cover with plastic wrap and marinate for 20 minutes at room temperature, turning several times in the marinade.

3. Remove the zucchini from the bowl and, using your hands, squeeze out the excess water. Toss the zucchini in the pesto. Arrange the zucchini shreds on a serving platter.

4. Prepare a medium-hot fire for grilling and place the grill rack about 3 inches above the coals. Arrange the halibut on the grill rack and grill until cooked through, basting several times with the marinade, 5 to 7 minutes on each side. Remove the cooked fillets and cut them in half across the length.

5. Arrange the fish on top of the zucchini. Drizzle the dressing on top. To eat, scoop some of the grilled fish and zucchini onto a warm tortilla, roll up, and eat with your fingers.

MAKES 6 SERVINGS

Grilled Swordfish Kebabs with Pineapple Salsa

I have to credit my friend and fellow cook Chris Schlesinger, of the East Coast Grill and coauthor of *The Thrill of the Grill* and *License to Grill*, with introducing me to the tantalizing flavors of grilled seafood and how good they are paired with myriad salsas. In this dish, the pineapple salsa complements the grilled seafood beautifully.

1½ pounds swordfish steaks, skin removed and cut into chunks about 1½ inches square

FOR THE MARINADE, mixed together:
¼ cup rice wine or sake
2 tablespoons soy sauce
1 tablespoon peeled and minced fresh ginger
1 teaspoon toasted sesame oil

Ten 10-inch-long bamboo skewers, soaked in water to cover for 1 hour and drained

TO SERVE:
2 to 3 heads Boston lettuce, cores trimmed, leaves separated, pressed to flatten, rinsed, drained, and arranged on a serving platter or in a basket, or 18 flour tortillas, brushed lightly with toasted sesame oil, folded into quarters, steamed for 10 minutes, arranged in a basket or serving bowl, and covered with a dish towel to keep warm
Pineapple Salsa (page 144)

1. Put the fish in a medium-size bowl. Add the marinade and toss lightly to coat. Cover with plastic wrap and marinate for 20 minutes at room temperature, turning the fish several times in the marinade.

2. Thread the fish onto the skewers and set aside.

3. Prepare a medium-hot fire for grilling and place the grill rack about 3 inches above the coals. Arrange the kebabs on the grill rack and cook until cooked through, basting once or twice with the marinade, 4 to 5 minutes on each side. Remove the fish from the skewers and arrange on a serving platter.

4. To eat, put a chunk or two in the center of a lettuce leaf, spoon some of the pineapple salsa on top, roll up, and eat with your fingers.

MAKES 6 SERVINGS

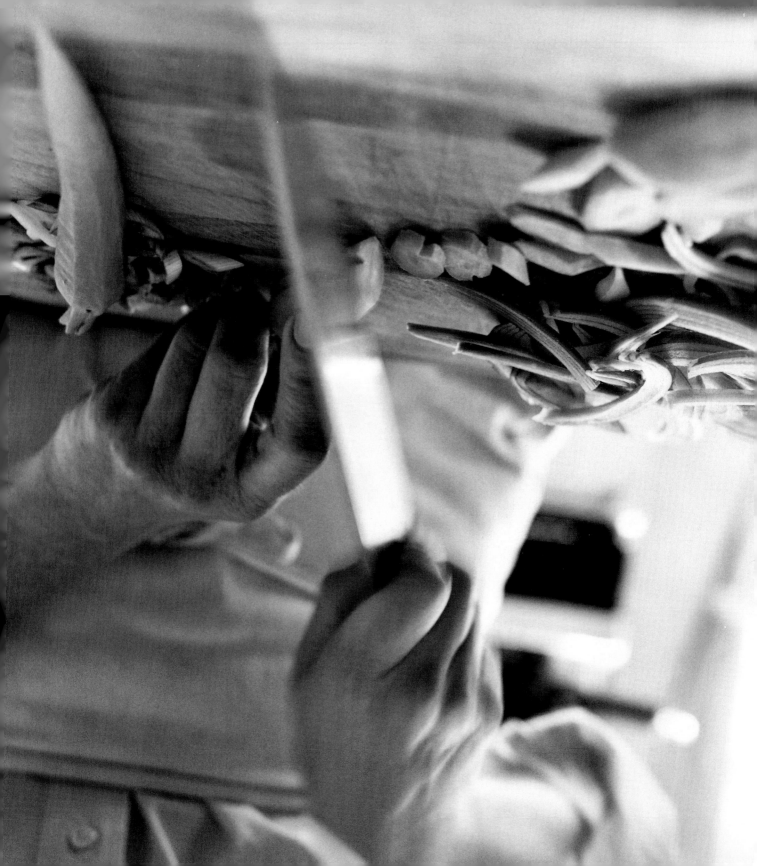

Vegetarian
Wraps

Rainbow Vegetables with Spicy Sesame Dressing ❧ Spicy Vegetable Curry ❧ Barbecued Tofu Wraps ❧ Tofu Sambal ❧ Fried Wild Mushroom Rice Wraps ❧ Grilled Tempeh with Basil ❧ Singapore Noodles in Lettuce Leaves ❧

When I was a student in the seventies, one of the most memorable pleasures of being in Asia was discovering the extraordinary world of Chinese, Malaysian, Japanese, Korean, Indian, Thai, and Vietnamese vegetarian cooking. Unlike the bland and insipid dishes I had come to associate with Western meatless dishes, Asian vegetarian food was absolutely electric. The flavors were vibrant and diverse. I simply couldn't get enough.

Myriad seasonings like garlic, ginger, fresh herbs, black mushrooms, and toasted sesame oil are basic to the Asian vegetarian pantry, as are legions of fresh vegetables and all forms of tofu and tempeh, a fermented soy cake.

I dare anyone to try the dishes in this chapter and not be intrigued. Spicy Vegetable Curry is a sumptuous dish laced with hot peppers, oregano, fennel, turmeric, and cumin. Stuffed into Indian flatbreads or pita, it makes a truly satisfying meal. For Barbecued Tofu Wraps and Grilled Tempeh with Basil, the tofu or tempeh is first marinated in enticing mixtures pungent with garlic and fresh ginger, then charcoal-grilled before being tossed with crisp-cooked vegetables. My father was astounded when he tasted these dishes. After seventy-eight years of being a diehard carnivore, he raved about the grilled tempeh stir-fried with red onions and basil, admitting that it tasted (dare I say it?) "just like pork."

The recipes on the following pages prove that vegetarian dishes can be just as sumptuous and satisfying as those with meat. And that's not even considering their impressive health benefits.

Rainbow Vegetables with Spicy Sesame Dressing

This spicy sesame dressing is a variation of one of my most requested recipes, a spicy peanut sauce. In this recipe, I substitute toasted sesame paste, which is sold in Asian markets, for the peanut butter. Do not substitute tahini paste. The dressing is also delicious on salads and noodles. Here it is wonderful drizzled liberally over vegetables served in lettuce leaves.

3 cups grated carrots

2 cups peeled, seeded, and grated English seedless or Kirby cucumbers

2 cups bean sprouts, rinsed and drained

2 medium-size red bell peppers, cored, seeded, and cut into thin julienne strips

1 medium-size yellow bell pepper, cored, seeded, and cut into thin julienne strips

FOR THE SPICY SESAME DRESSING:

8 cloves garlic, peeled

Two 1-inch-square pieces fresh ginger, peeled

1 teaspoon crushed red pepper

6 tablespoons Chinese toasted sesame paste (mix well before adding), or more as needed

1/4 cup toasted sesame oil

5 tablespoons soy sauce

1/4 cup rice wine or sake

1 1/2 tablespoons Chinese black vinegar or Worcestershire sauce

1 1/2 tablespoons sugar

6 tablespoons water, or more as needed

TO SERVE:

2 heads Boston lettuce, cores trimmed, leaves separated, pressed to flatten, rinsed, drained, and arranged in a serving bowl or basket

1. Arrange the carrots, cucumbers, bean sprouts, and red and yellow pepper strips in mounds or separate concentric circles on a serving platter.

2. To prepare the dressing, in a food processor fitted with the steel blade or in a blender, process the garlic and ginger until finely chopped. Add the remaining dressing ingredients in the order they are listed and process until smooth. The dressing should be the consistency of heavy cream. If it is too thick, add more broth or water; if too thin, add more sesame paste. Pour into a serving container. (The dressing will keep refrigerated for up to 1 month.)

3. To eat, spoon some of the shredded vegetables onto a leaf of lettuce, drizzle some sesame dressing on top, roll up, tucking in the edges, and eat with your fingers.

MAKES 6 SERVINGS

Spicy Vegetable Curry

This sumptuous curry is redolent of seasonings like turmeric, fennel, oregano, garlic, and ginger. It's such a satisfying and filling dish that even hard-core carnivores will not notice the absence of meat.

1½ pounds firm tofu, cut through the thickness into 1-inch-thick slices

2½ tablespoons safflower or corn oil

FOR THE SEASONINGS, mixed together:

1½ tablespoons minced garlic (5 to 6 cloves)

1½ tablespoons peeled and minced fresh ginger

1 teaspoon crushed red pepper, or to taste

1 teaspoon turmeric

1 teaspoon fennel seeds

1 teaspoon dried oregano

1 teaspoon ground coriander

1 teaspoon ground cumin

TO FINISH THE CURRY:

2 medium-size onions, coarsely chopped (about 1½ cups)

5 medium-size ripe tomatoes, peeled, seeded, and diced, or one 28-ounce can whole tomatoes, seeded and diced

¾ cup unsweetened coconut milk (mix well before using)

1 pound cauliflower, cut into 1-inch chunks and florets

2 cups fresh or thawed frozen peas

1 teaspoon salt, or to taste

¼ cup coarsely chopped dry-roasted peanuts

TO SERVE:

Indian Flatbread (page 16) or 16 squares lavash bread or pita pocket halves, arranged in a basket

1. Wrap the tofu slices in paper towels or a cotton dish towel and place a heavy weight, such as a cast-iron skillet, on top. Let stand for 30 minutes to press out the excess water, then cut into ½-inch dice.

2. Heat a large casserole or Dutch oven over high heat until very hot. Add the oil and heat until hot, about 20 seconds. Add the seasonings and stir-fry until fragrant, about 10 seconds. Reduce the heat to low, add the onions, and cook, stirring, until soft and translucent, about 4 minutes.

3. Add the tomatoes and coconut milk and cook, partially covered, for 5 to 7 minutes. Add the tofu dice and cauliflower and cook, covered, until the cauliflower is almost tender, 16 to 18 minutes.

4. Add the peas and salt, cover, and cook for about 3 minutes, stirring once. Transfer to a platter. Sprinkle with the chopped peanuts. To eat, spoon some of the curry onto the Indian flatbread, lavash, or pita, roll up, and eat with your fingers.

MAKES 6 SERVINGS

Barbecued Tofu Wraps

Grilling tofu changes its texture subtly, so that even those who are hesitant have warmed to this dish. The garlicky hoisin sauce marinade helps to make this one of the most popular vegetarian dishes I prepare.

2 pounds firm tofu, cut through
    the thickness into 1-inch-thick
    slices

FOR THE BARBECUE MARINADE:
¾ cup hoisin sauce
¼ cup rice wine or sake
3 tablespoons soy sauce
1½ tablespoons very finely minced
    garlic

Five 10-inch-long bamboo skewers,
    soaked in water to cover for
    1 hour and drained

FOR THE VEGETABLES:
1 tablespoon safflower or corn oil
1 tablespoon minced garlic
1 teaspoon hot chili paste or
    crushed red pepper
1 large red bell pepper, cored,
    seeded, and cut into thin
    julienne strips
1 large yellow bell pepper, cored,
    seeded, and cut into thin
    julienne strips
½ pound fresh snow peas, ends
    snapped and veiny strings
    removed
1½ tablespoons rice wine or sake
2 cups scallion greens cut into
    ½-inch lengths

FOR THE SAUCE, mixed together:
3½ tablespoons soy sauce
1½ tablespoons sugar
1 teaspoon toasted sesame oil

TO SERVE:
18 Steamed Lotus Buns (page 14)
    or flour tortillas, brushed lightly
    with toasted sesame oil, folded
    into quarters, steamed for 10
    minutes, arranged in a basket
    or a serving bowl, and covered
    with a dish towel to keep warm

1. Cut the tofu into 1½-inch cubes. Place the cubes in a bowl.

2. Add two thirds of the marinade to the tofu, tossing to coat. Let sit for an hour at room temperature.

3. Thread the tofu onto the skewers, reserving the remaining marinade in the bowl for basting.

4. Prepare a medium-hot fire for grilling or preheat the broiler. Place the skewered tofu about 3 inches from the heat source and cook for 8 to 9 minutes on each side, turning once, basting occasionally with the marinade. Remove the tofu from the skewers and cut into slices ½ inch thick and 2 inches long.

5. Heat a wok or a large heavy skillet over high heat. Add the oil and heat until very hot. Add the minced garlic, chili paste or crushed red pepper, and bell peppers and toss lightly for about 1 minute. Add the snow peas and rice wine and continue cooking, tossing lightly, until the snow peas are tender, 2 to 3 minutes. Add the scallions and sauce and toss lightly to coat.

6. Spoon the vegetables onto a serving platter. Arrange the barbecued tofu slices on top and pour the reserved barbecue marinade on top. To eat, spoon some of the stir-fried mixture onto a lotus bun or a flour tortilla, roll in the edges of the bun or roll up the tortilla, and eat with your fingers.

MAKES 6 SERVINGS

Tofu Sambal

I was first introduced to sambals in Penang, where I was served juicy prawns drenched in an intoxicating sauce made with garlic, cumin, turmeric, ginger, and coconut milk. I started experimenting and found that many foods are equally delicious served this way—especially tofu. (You can use light coconut milk for fewer calories.)

1½ pounds firm tofu, cut through the thickness into ½-inch-thick slices

FOR THE SEASONINGS:

3 dried chili peppers, seeds removed, or 1½ teaspoons crushed red pepper
Two ½-inch-thick slices peeled fresh ginger
6 cloves garlic, peeled
1½ teaspoons ground cumin
½ teaspoon turmeric

FOR THE VEGETABLES:

2 quarts water
¾ pound snow peas, ends trimmed, veiny strings removed, and sliced lengthwise in half
2 tablespoons safflower or corn oil
1½ red onions, cut into thin julienne strips

FOR THE COCONUT SAUCE, mixed together:

1 cup unsweetened coconut milk (mix well before using)

1 tablespoon firmly packed light brown sugar
1 teaspoon salt

2 tablespoons freshly squeezed lime juice, or to taste

TO SERVE:

Indian Flatbread (page 16) or 18 squares lavash bread or pita pocket halves, arranged in a basket

1. Wrap the tofu slices in paper towels or a cotton dish towel and place a heavy weight, such as a cast-iron skillet, on top. Let stand for 30 minutes to press out the excess water, then cut into ½-inch dice.

2. While the machine is running, drop the seasonings, in the order listed, into a blender or the feed tube of a food processor fitted with the steel blade and process to a paste. Turn the machine on and off several times to get a smooth mixture.

3. Bring the water to a boil in a medium-size saucepan. Add the snow peas, blanch for 15 seconds. Drain in a colander, refresh under cold running water, and drain again.

4. Heat a large heavy saucepan over high heat until very hot. Add the oil and heat until hot, about 30 seconds. Add the seasoning paste and cook over medium heat, stirring with a wooden spoon, until fragrant, 6 to 7 minutes.

5. Add the onions and toss until soft, about 1½ minutes. Add the coconut sauce and heat until boiling. Add the tofu cubes, partially cover, and cook for about 10 minutes.

6. Stir in the lime juice and spoon the sambal into a serving bowl. To eat, spoon some of the sambal onto a flatbread, lavash, or pita, roll up, and eat with your fingers.

MAKES 6 SERVINGS

Fried Wild Mushroom Rice Wraps

I love to serve these delectable fried rice wraps for hors d'oeuvres or as an unusual light meal. They are especially convenient for entertaining, because they can be prepared in advance and served chilled or at room temperature.

1. Bring the water to a boil in a large pot. Add the cabbage leaves and blanch for 4 seconds. Remove and refresh under cold running water. Drain thoroughly on paper towels and arrange around the edges of a serving platter.

2. Heat a wok or a large heavy skillet over high heat until very hot. Add the oil and heat until hot. Add the garlic and mushrooms and stir-fry until slightly softened, 1 to 2 minutes. Reduce the heat to medium-high and add the rice wine. Partially cover and cook until the mushrooms are tender, about 3½ minutes. Uncover, add the scallions, and cook to reduce the liquid by half.

3. Add the rice, breaking it up with a spatula. Cook until heated through, 2 to 3 minutes. Add the soy sauce, 1½ tablespoons water, salt, and black pepper and toss lightly to blend. Add the cilantro and toss to mix.

4. Spoon the rice into the center of the serving platter. Put the sauce in small bowl. To eat, spoon some of the rice mixture onto a cabbage leaf, roll up, tucking in the edges, dip in the dipping sauce, and eat with your fingers.

MAKES 6 SERVINGS

3 quarts water
1 medium-size head Chinese (Napa) cabbage, leaves separated, pressed to flatten, and stems trimmed
2 tablespoons safflower or corn oil
8 cloves garlic, smashed with the flat side of a cleaver and very thinly sliced
½ pound fresh shiitake mushrooms, wiped clean, stems removed, and caps thinly sliced
½ pound fresh cremini mushrooms, wiped clean, stems removed, and caps thinly sliced
3 tablespoons rice wine or sake
2 cups minced scallion greens
4 cups cooked rice, chilled, then separated with a fork
3½ tablespoons soy sauce
1½ tablespoons water
½ teaspoon salt
½ teaspoon freshly ground black pepper
¼ cup chopped cilantro (fresh coriander) leaves
Spicy Korean Dipping Sauce (page 151)

Grilled Tempeh with Basil

You'll adore the flavor of this sumptuous stir-fry, with its fresh flavorings of garlic, red onion, and holy basil. Once marinated and grilled, the tempeh tastes quite similar to meat. Holy basil, or graprao basil, has small, purplish leaves and a slight licorice flavor. It is used in stir-fried dishes and salads. If it is unavailable, substitute sweet basil. The saltiness of fish sauces varies, so season to taste.

1½ pounds soy tempeh

FOR THE MARINADE, mixed together:
3 tablespoons soy sauce
1½ tablespoons rice wine or sake
1½ tablespoons minced shallots
1 teaspoon toasted sesame oil

1½ tablespoons safflower or corn
    oil (you will need an additional
    teaspoon of oil if you sear the
    tempeh in a pan)

FOR THE SEASONINGS:
1½ tablespoons fresh red chili
    pepper, ends trimmed, seeds
    removed, and chopped

2 tablespoons chopped garlic
3 medium-size red onions, cut into
    thin julienne strips

FOR THE SAUCE, mixed together:
3 tablespoons fish sauce, or to taste
1½ tablespoons soy sauce
1 tablespoon sugar
1½ tablespoons water

TO FINISH:
1½ cups fresh Thai holy basil or
    sweet basil leaves, stems
    trimmed, rinsed, drained, and
    coarsely shredded

TO SERVE:
18 Steamed Lotus Buns (page 14)
    or flour tortillas, brushed lightly
    with toasted sesame oil, folded
    into quarters, steamed for 10
    minutes, arranged in a basket
    or a serving bowl, and covered
    with a dish towel to keep warm

1. Put the tempeh in a bowl, add the marinade, and toss gently to coat. Let marinate for 20 minutes.

2. Prepare a medium-hot fire for grilling or heat a large heavy skillet for searing. Place the grill rack 3 inches above the coals, arrange the tempeh on the rack, and grill for 3 to 4 minutes per side. Or, add 1 teaspoon oil to the pan, heat until hot, and sear the tempeh on each side for 2 to 3 minutes. Remove, let cool slightly, and cut on the diagonal into thin slices.

3. Heat a wok or a large heavy skillet over high heat until very hot. Add the oil and heat until very hot, about 30 seconds. Add the seasonings and stir-fry, tossing, until the onions are tender, 1½ to 2 minutes. Give the sauce a stir, add it to the pan, and bring to a boil. Add the cooked tempeh and the basil and mix.

4. Scoop the tempeh onto a serving platter. To eat, spoon some of the stir-fried mixture onto a lotus bun or flour tortilla, roll it up, tucking in the edges, and eat with your fingers.

MAKES 6 SERVINGS

Singapore Noodles in Lettuce Leaves

Singapore, with its numerous hawker stands, is noodle heaven, and one of the most traditional dishes is rice noodles studded with flash-cooked vegetables and shrimp and dusted with curry powder. This vegetarian version, which is also seasoned generously with garlic and ginger, is both colorful and delicious.

2 tablespoons safflower or corn oil

FOR THE SEASONINGS, mixed together:

1½ tablespoons minced garlic

1 tablespoon peeled and minced fresh ginger

1½ tablespoons curry powder, preferably Madras curry

FOR THE VEGETABLES:

2½ cups very thinly sliced red onions (about 2 onions)

2 cups thin julienne strips red bell peppers (about 2 medium-size peppers)

3 cups cored and thinly sliced Chinese (Napa) cabbage

FOR THE SAUCE, mixed together:

¼ cup water

3 tablespoons soy sauce

1 teaspoon salt

½ teaspoon sugar

¼ teaspoon freshly ground black pepper

TO FINISH:

⅓ pound thin rice stick noodles or vermicelli, softened in hot water and drained

TO SERVE:

2 heads Boston lettuce, cores trimmed, leaves separated, pressed to flatten, rinsed, drained, and arranged around the edges of a serving bowl or deep platter

1. Heat a wok or a large heavy skillet over high heat until very hot. Add the oil and heat until very hot, about 30 seconds. Add the seasonings and stir-fry until fragrant, about 10 seconds.

2. Add the red onions and stir-fry until just tender, about 2 minutes. Add the red peppers and toss lightly for a minute, then add the cabbage and continue cooking until the vegetables are crisp-tender, about 3 minutes. Add the sauce mixture and the softened noodles and carefully toss to blend. Cook until the noodles are tender, about a minute, then transfer the noodles to a serving dish.

3. To eat, spoon some of the noodle mixture onto a lettuce leaf, roll it up, tucking in the edges, and eat with your fingers.

MAKES 6 SERVINGS

Salsas, Sauces, Dressings, Chutneys, and Slaws

Spicy Salsa ❧ Pineapple Salsa ❧ Mango Salsa ❧ Peanut Sauce ❧ Saté Sauce ❧ Soy Dipping Sauce ❧ Smoked Salmon Sushi Dipping Sauce ❧ Spicy Korean Dipping Sauce ❧ Vietnamese Sweet-and-Sour Dipping Sauce ❧ Korean Sesame Dressing ❧ Chili-Garlic Dressing ❧ Indonesian Peanut-Coconut Dressing ❧ Fresh Cilantro Vinaigrette ❧ Mango Chutney ❧ Asian Slaw ❧

Sauces are integral to any cuisine, but they are especially important in Asia, where the difference between a simple dish and a delicacy is very often in the sauce or dressing. Consider the plight of a dumpling without its accompaniment of soy sauce, black vinegar, and fine shreds or minced bits of fresh ginger. Or a naked Vietnamese spring roll without *nuoc cham,* a masterful blending of fresh lime juice, fish sauce, hot pepper, sugar, and garlic. The sauce raises the food to a higher and ultimately more delectable dimension.

The repertoire of Asian sauces is considerable, yet the ingredients are modest and many of the condiments overlap boundaries. The most basic are soy sauce, fish sauce, rice wine or sake, mirin (sweetened rice wine), rice vinegars, fresh lemon and lime juices, toasted sesame oil, and the seasonings garlic, fresh ginger, scallions, cilantro, basil, and mint, among others. Fortunately, thanks to the ever-widening international section in mainstream supermarkets, these condiments are now widely available. If you need to make a minor substitution, go right ahead. Although you may subtly alter the tone of the sauce, rest assured, it will still maintain its integrity.

There are other side dishes that often make a food whole—salsas, chutneys, and side salads or slaws. These dishes play an especially significant role in the "New Asian" recipes. For instance, barbecued pork is quite tasty by itself, but it becomes sensational accompanied by Asian Slaw. Chinese Jerk Chicken is delicious on its own, but if it is slathered with some Mango Chutney in a flour tortilla wrap, its flavor is elevated to outstanding. And the grilled shrimp are excellent, but they become memorable with a fresh cilantro-tomato salsa.

Many of these sauces, salsas, dressings, and chutneys will keep for some time, so I like to make large quantities to keep on hand in the refrigerator. They are especially good with grilled seafood, meat, and vegetables. Feel free to pair them with other recipes or sprinkle in fresh herbs and seasonings of your choice.

Spicy Salsa

Tomatoes are relatively new to China, but chefs are now using them in all kinds of dishes. I love tomatoes—cooked and raw—especially in this vibrantly seasoned salsa. I particularly like it with grilled seafood and chicken.

1. Combine the jalapeños and garlic in a blender or a food processor fitted with the steel blade and process to a smooth paste. Add the minced scallions and blend to a rough mixture. Add the tomatoes and pulse until finely chopped.

2. Transfer to a serving bowl and stir in the lemon juice, cilantro, and salt. Taste for seasoning, adding more salt if necessary. Cover with plastic wrap and let sit for 30 minutes at room temperature, then refrigerate until ready to serve. Refrigerated, this will keep in a tightly covered container for up to a week.

MAKES ABOUT 1½ CUPS

1 to 2 jalapeño peppers, to your taste, ends trimmed and seeds removed
1 tablespoon minced garlic
1 cup minced scallion greens
1 pound ripe tomatoes, rinsed, drained, cored, and cut into chunks
Juice of 1 lemon
½ cup cilantro (fresh coriander) leaves, coarsely chopped
1 teaspoon salt, or more to taste

Pineapple Salsa

Tropical fruits such as pineapple, papaya, and mango are superb in tart salsas and chutneys. They provide a wonderful, contrasting flavor counterpoint to char-grilled seafood and chicken.

1 ripe pineapple

2 medium-size red bell peppers, cored, seeded, and cut into ¼-inch dice

1 medium-size red onion, minced

1 teaspoon ground cumin, or to taste

Juice of 2 limes (about 6 tablespoons)

¼ cup orange or pineapple juice

⅓ cup chopped cilantro (fresh coriander) leaves

Salt and freshly ground black pepper

1. Remove and discard the core from the pineapple, then peel and cut the pineapple into ¼-inch dice. Put in a large bowl and add the red peppers and onion. Add the cumin, lime juice, and orange or pineapple juice and season to taste, adding the cilantro, salt, and pepper.

2. Spoon into a serving dish and serve at room temperature. Refrigerated, this will keep in a tightly covered container for several days.

MAKES ABOUT 5 CUPS

Mango Salsa

This luscious mango salsa, with its seasonings of fresh lime juice, hot chilies, and fresh cilantro, is colorful and versatile. I serve it with all types of grilled seafood and chicken. I often substitute papayas and peaches for the mangoes.

3 to 4 ripe mangoes, peeled, seeded, and cut into ¼-inch dice
1 medium-size red onion, minced
1 teaspoon ground cumin
Juice of 2 limes (about 6 tablespoons)
¼ cup chopped cilantro (fresh coriander) leaves
1 teaspoon salt
¼ teaspoon freshly ground black pepper

1. In a medium-size bowl, mix together the mangoes and onion. Add the cumin and lime juice and season to taste, adding the cilantro, salt, and pepper.

2. Spoon into a serving dish and serve at room temperature. This will keep refrigerated for 3 to 4 days.

MAKES ABOUT 3 CUPS

Peanut Sauce

This Vietnamese peanut sauce is truly superb with spring rolls and as an all-purpose dipping sauce for hors d'oeuvres. The ingredients may sound unusual, but once cooked, they all blend to create a delicious, all-purpose condiment.

1. In a small bowl, combine the peanut butter, tomato paste, hoisin sauce, sugar, and water, blending until smooth.

2. Heat a small heavy saucepan over medium-high heat. Add the oil and heat until hot, then add the garlic and crushed red pepper and fry for about 5 seconds. Add the peanut butter mixture, stir to blend, and continue cooking for 3 to 4 minutes until thickened.

3. Remove from the heat, let cool slightly, and serve warm or at room temperature. Refrigerated, the sauce will keep in a tightly covered container for up to a week.

MAKES ABOUT ¾ CUP

2 tablespoons smooth peanut butter
1½ teaspoons tomato paste
¼ cup hoisin sauce
1 teaspoon sugar
⅓ cup water
1 teaspoon safflower or corn oil
1½ teaspoons minced garlic
1 teaspoon crushed red pepper

Saté Sauce

Saté, which is thin slices of grilled chicken or meat served with a coconut-peanut sauce, originated in Indonesia but has traveled widely across borders to other Asian countries; Malaysians, Indians, and Chinese all have their versions. The two common ingredients in the sauce are peanuts and coconut milk. Here is my interpretation of this classic, sumptuous sauce.

¾ cup smooth peanut butter

1¼ cups unsweetened coconut milk
  (mix well before adding)

3 tablespoons fish sauce

3 tablespoons peeled and minced
  fresh ginger

3 tablespoons firmly packed light
  brown sugar

1 tablespoon soy sauce

1 teaspoon crushed red pepper

1. In a blender or a food processor fitted with the steel blade, process the ingredients together until smooth.

2. Transfer to a serving container and serve at room temperature. Refrigerated, the sauce will keep in a tightly covered container for at least 5 days.

MAKES ABOUT 2½ CUPS

Soy Dipping Sauce

A dumpling would not be the same without a dipping sauce, and often each Asian cook has his or her own interpretation. Here's a basic sauce for Chinese ground pork dumplings, with two variations.

1. Combine all the ingredients in a small bowl.
2. Transfer to a serving dish and use at room temperature. Refrigerated, the sauce will keep in a tightly covered container for up to a week.

VARIATION I: Substitute 2 tablespoons peeled and finely shredded fresh ginger for the garlic and add 3 tablespoons Chinese black vinegar or Worcestershire sauce.

VARIATION II: Add 1 teaspoon hot chili paste and 1½ tablespoons sugar for additional heat.

MAKES 1 CUP

¾ cup soy sauce
1 tablespoon minced garlic
¼ cup water

Smoked Salmon Sushi Dipping Sauce

Sushi is commonly served with soy sauce and wasabi, but this lemony dipping sauce complements the smoked salmon sushi on page 50 superbly.

½ cup soy sauce
juice of 1 lemon (5 to 6 tablespoons)
½ cup water

1. In a small bowl, mix all of the ingredients together well.

2. Transfer to a serving dish and serve at room temperature. Refrigerated, the sauce will keep in a tightly covered container for up to a week.

MAKES ABOUT 1 ¼ CUPS

Spicy Korean Dipping Sauce

Like many Asians, Koreans love hot chili peppers, but they particularly love them in combination with other pungent seasonings such as ginger, rice vinegar, and sugar. The flavors marry and make a delicious, multidimensional dipping sauce that is served with dumplings and steamed rolls.

1. In a small bowl, mix all of the ingredients together well.

2. Transfer to a serving dish and serve at room temperature. Refrigerated, the sauce will keep in a tightly covered container for up to a week.

MAKES ABOUT 1 CUP

Note: To toast sesame seeds, fry in a dry frying pan over medium-low heat, stirring occasionally, until golden brown.

½ cup soy sauce
3½ tablespoons Japanese rice vinegar
1½ tablespoons peeled and minced fresh ginger
2 teaspoons sugar
2 teaspoons toasted sesame seeds (see Note)
1 teaspoon crushed red pepper or 1½ teaspoons Korean red pepper powder (available at Asian specialty markets)
2 tablespoons water

Vietnamese Sweet-and-Sour Dipping Sauce

In Vietnamese, this is called *nuoc cham,* and it's delightfully light and fresh. I make several times the recipe and have it on hand to use as a versatile salad dressing or a dipping sauce for dumplings.

1 teaspoon crushed red pepper
Juice of 3 limes or 2 lemons
1 tablespoon minced garlic
3 tablespoons sugar
¼ cup fish sauce
2 tablespoons grated carrots

1. Soak the crushed red pepper in the citrus juice for several minutes. Add the garlic, sugar, and fish sauce and stir to dissolve the sugar.

2. Transfer to a serving container, add the grated carrots, and serve at room temperature. Refrigerated, the sauce will keep in a tightly covered container for up to 5 days.

MAKES ABOUT ⅔ CUP

Korean Sesame Dressing

Toasted sesame oil can have a strident, if not domineering, flavor, but it becomes balanced with the addition of Japanese rice vinegar, garlic, soy sauce, and chili paste. This is an unusual and delicious salad dressing.

5 tablespoons Japanese rice vinegar
31/2 tablespoons toasted sesame oil
3 tablespoons sweetened rice wine
   (mirin)
2 tablespoons soy sauce
1 tablespoon sugar
2 tablespoon minced garlic
2 teaspoons hot chili paste, or to taste
1/4 cup crushed toasted sesame seeds
   (see Note on page 151)

1. Combine all the ingredients, stirring to dissolve the sugar.

2. Transfer to a serving dish and serve at room temperature. Refrigerated, the dressing will keep in a tightly covered container for up to a week.

MAKES ABOUT 1 1/4 CUPS

Chili-Garlic Dressing

This pungent dressing is delicious on meat, seafood, or plain vegetable salads. For a fresh variation, substitute freshly squeezed lemon juice to taste for the Japanese rice vinegar.

¼ cup safflower or corn oil

2½ tablespoons toasted sesame oil

1 teaspoon crushed red pepper or 4 to 6 small dried chili peppers, cut into ¼-inch lengths and seeds removed

1½ tablespoons minced garlic

1 tablespoon peeled and minced fresh ginger

7 tablespoons soy sauce

2 tablespoons rice wine or sake

1½ tablespoons sugar

3 tablespoons Chinese black vinegar or Worcestershire sauce

1. Combine the oils in a small heavy saucepan with a lid and heat until near smoking over high heat. Add the red pepper or chilies, cover, and remove the pan from the heat. Add the garlic and ginger and let cool, then add the remaining ingredients. Stir to blend and dissolve the sugar.

2. Transfer to a serving container and serve at room temperature. Refrigerated, the dressing will keep in a tightly covered container for up to a week.

MAKES ABOUT 1½ CUPS

Indonesian Peanut-Coconut Dressing

I have always enjoyed this sumptuous dressing served with the Indonesian salad known as *gado gado*. I make a large batch and use it liberally on cold noodles, myriad salads, and grilled vegetables.

2 small fresh red or jalapeño peppers, ends trimmed and seeds removed, or 1½ teaspoons crushed red pepper

4 shallots, peeled

3 cloves garlic, peeled

¾ cup crunchy peanut butter

1 cup unsweetened coconut milk (mix well before using)

2 tablespoons firmly packed light brown sugar

2 tablespoons fish sauce

2 teaspoons tamarind pulp, dissolved in ¼ cup water, or 3 tablespoons freshly squeezed lemon juice

1. With the machine running, drop the peppers, shallots, and garlic through the feed tube of a food processor fitted with the steel blade and puree. Add the remaining ingredients to the bowl, one at a time, in the order in which they are listed, pulsing after each addition until you have a smooth paste.

2. Pour the mixture into a saucepan and cook over low heat, stirring occasionally, until it has thickened, 5 to 6 minutes.

3. Pour into a serving dish and serve warm. Refrigerated, the dressing will keep in a tightly covered container for up to a month.

MAKES ABOUT 2 CUPS

Fresh Cilantro Vinaigrette

Cilantro has a strong musky flavor, but it is beautifully suited to dressings with rice vinegar and soy sauce, which balance its flavor. You can prepare this dressing quite a bit in advance, but add the cilantro just before serving to preserve its fresh green color. This is particularly delicious with grilled seafood and chicken.

1. In a small bowl, combine all the ingredients except the cilantro, stirring to dissolve the sugar.

2. Transfer to a serving container, sprinkle in the cilantro, and serve at room temperature. Refrigerated, the dressing will keep in a tightly covered container for several days.

MAKES ABOUT 1 CUP

⅓ cup soy sauce
¼ cup Japanese rice vinegar
2½ tablespoons toasted sesame oil
Juice of ½ lemon (2½ to 3 tablespoons)
1½ tablespoons rice wine or sake
1½ tablespoons sugar
1 teaspoon salt
6 tablespoons chopped cilantro (fresh coriander) leaves

Mango Chutney

The secret to this chutney is that the mangoes *must* be unripe and green; otherwise, the cooked mixture will turn to mush. It is especially delicious with grilled meats, seafood, and stews.

FOR THE SPICE PASTE:
5 cloves garlic, peeled
One 1-inch piece fresh ginger, peeled
2 small fresh red chili peppers, ends
    trimmed and seeds removed
1 teaspoon ground cumin
1 teaspoon ground coriander
½ teaspoon turmeric
2 tablespoons corn or safflower oil

1 cinnamon stick
2 stars anise

FOR THE CHUTNEY:
3 green, unripe mangoes (total weight
    about 3 pounds), peeled, seeded,
    and cut into ½-inch dice

FOR THE DRESSING, mixed together:
½ cup white vinegar
¼ cup sugar, or more to taste if the
    mangoes are very sour
1½ teaspoons salt, or to taste
2 tablespoons raisins

1. In a food processor fitted with the steel blade or a blender, with the machine running, add the garlic, ginger, chilies, cumin, coriander, and turmeric, in that order, through the feed tube and process to a smooth paste, adding a little of the oil if necessary.

2. Heat a saucepan over medium-high heat, add the remaining oil, and heat until hot. Add the spice paste and the whole spices and cook, stirring frequently, over medium-low heat until very fragrant, 6 to 7 minutes.

3. Add the mangoes and dressing mixture to the seasonings and stir. Reduce the heat to low and cook until the mangoes are soft, about 30 minutes. Remove from the heat and serve hot or cold. Refrigerated, the chutney will keep for up to a month in a tightly covered container.

MAKES ABOUT 3 CUPS

Asian Slaw

I adore hot-and-sour pickles, slaws, and salads. This is one of the most basic, but you can substitute cucumbers, summer squashes, or other types of Western and Chinese cabbage for the Napa. It can be served warm, at room temperature, or cold.

1. Separate the cabbage leaves. Trim away the stem ends and leafy tip ends and discard. Rinse thoroughly and drain. With a sharp knife, cut the leaves crosswise into julienne strips about ½ inch wide, separating the stem sections from the leafy sections.

2. Heat a wok or a large heavy skillet over high heat until very hot. Add the oil and heat until hot, about 20 seconds. Add the crushed red pepper and minced ginger and stir-fry for about 15 seconds. Add the red pepper dice and stir-fry for about 30 seconds, then add the rice wine and continue stir-frying for another 30 seconds. Add the stem sections of the cabbage and the grated carrots, toss lightly, and cook for a minute. Add the leafy sections, toss lightly, and pour on the dressing. Continue tossing lightly to coat and cook for about 30 seconds. Transfer to a serving bowl. Serve warm, at room temperature, or chilled. Refrigerated, this will keep in a tightly covered container for up to a week.

MAKES 6 SERVINGS

1 small head Chinese (Napa) cabbage (about 1½ pounds)
1 tablespoon canola or corn oil
1 teaspoon crushed red pepper
2½ tablespoons peeled and minced fresh ginger
1 medium-size red bell pepper, cored, seeded, and cut into ¼-inch dice
1½ tablespoons rice wine or sake
2 medium-size carrots, grated (about 1½ cups)

FOR THE HOT-AND-SOUR DRESSING, mixed together:

3 tablespoons soy sauce
½ teaspoon salt
2 tablespoons sugar
2½ tablespoons Chinese black vinegar or Worcestershire sauce

Index

*G*ado gado, 55, 70, 156
ginger-teriyaki sauce, for grilled
    ginger chicken, 82
grilled:
    ginger chicken, 82
    lamb with flash-cooked fennel,
        100–102
    miso salmon with sweet-and-sour
        cucumbers, 78, 80
    shrimp with fresh salsa, 116
    swordfish kebabs with pineapple
        salsa, 120
    tempeh with basil, 125, 134
gyoza skins, 8, 32
    in Chinese meat dumplings, 32
    in steamed open-topped
        dumplings, 33

*H*alibut, barbecued, with spicy
    cilantro pesto, 118
hand-rolled sushi with smoked
    salmon, 50
hot-and-sour:
    dressing, for Asian slaw, 159
    sauce, 88
    slaw with shrimp, 65

*I*ceberg lettuce, 1, 8, 55
Indian, 125
    flatbreads, 8–9, 10, 16
    tandoori chicken with mango
        chutney, 110
    vegetable samosas, 37
Indonesian:
    peanut-coconut dressing, 156
    salad with coconut-peanut
        dressing, 55, 70

*J*affrey, Madhur, 16
Japanese, 24, 125
    basic sushi, 48–49
    hand-rolled sushi with smoked
        salmon, 50

soba bundles with chili-garlic
    dressing, 68
"jerk," 107

*K*orean, 125
    saucy, rolls, 77, 92
    sesame chicken salad, 60
    sesame dressing, 154
    spicy, dipping sauces, 151

*L*a lot, 1
lamb, grilled, with flash-cooked
    fennel, 100–102
lavash, 9, 10
leafy greens, 5, 8, 10, 56
leeks, flash-cooked chicken with,
    87
lemongrass beef wraps, 96
lemony Thai salad packages, 64
License to Grill (Schlesinger), 120
Lion's Head cabbage rolls, 77–78,
    94
lotus buns:
    for barbecued tofu wraps, 130
    for grilled tempeh with basil, 134
lotus leaves, 9, 10
    in lotus chicken packages, 46–47
lumpia wrappers, 5, 9, 10, 78
    in Cantonese spring rolls, 42
    in fresh Chinese spring rolls, 40

*M*alaysian, 8, 125
    pork rolls, 78, 93
Mandarin pancakes, 5, 8, 10, 12, 78
    in grilled lamb with flash-cooked
        fennel, 100–102
    in mu shu shrimp, 84–86
mango chutney, 141, 158
mango salsa, 146
    Chinese jerk chicken with, 109
marinades:
    for barbecued halibut with spicy
        cilantro pesto, 118

for barbecued pork loin with
    Asian slaw, 112
for barbecued sweet-and-sour
    shrimp, 26
for barbecued tofu wraps, 130
for Cantonese spring rolls, 42–43
for curried coconut chicken, 90
for flash-cooked chicken with
    leeks, 87
for grilled lamb with flash-
    cooked fennel, 100–102
for grilled miso salmon with
    sweet-and-sour cucumbers,
    80
for grilled shrimp with fresh
    salsa, 116
for grilled swordfish kebabs with
    pineapple salsa, 120
for grilled tempeh with basil, 134
for hot-and-sour scallops with
    broccoli, 88
for lemongrass beef wraps, 96
for lemony Thai salad packages,
    64
for lotus chicken packages, 46–47
for mu shu shrimp, 84–86
for pork saté with radicchio, 28
for seafood rice bundles, 66
for seared garlic beef with
    roasted rainbow peppers, 98
for seared steak with wild
    mushrooms, 114
for soba bundles with chili-garlic
    dressing, 68
for tandoori chicken with mango
    chutney, 110
Mexican, 9
    grilled shrimp with fresh salsa,
    116
mushrooms:
    fried wild, rice wraps, 133
    seared steak with wild, 114
mu shu shrimp, 84–86

Naan, 8–9, 16
Napa cabbage, 8, 10, 56
noodles:
 in sesame chicken salad, 60
 Singapore, in lettuce leaves, 136
 soba bundles with chili-garlic
  dressing, 68
 in Vietnamese spring rolls, 38
nori, 9, 10, 24
nuoc cham, 1, 141

Pancakes, Vietnamese shrimp, 83
pastes:
 jerk chicken, 109
 spice for mango chutney, 158
pastry:
 for flaky curry turnovers, 34–36
 for vegetable samosas, 37
peanut, peanut butter:
 dressing, 70
 in Indonesian peanut-coconut
  dressing, 156
 in saté sauce, 148
 sauce, 147
 for Vietnamese spring rolls, 38
pesto, spicy cilantro, 118
pineapple salsa, 144
 grilled swordfish kebabs with, 120
pita bread, 9, 10
pork:
 barbecued, loin with Asian slaw,
  112
 in Cantonese spring rolls, 42–43
 in Chinese meat dumplings, 32
 in lemony Thai salad packages,
  64
 in Lion's Head cabbage rolls,
  94
 Malaysian, rolls, 93
 saté with radicchio, 28
 in steamed open-topped
  dumplings, 33
purple laver, 9

Radicchio, 8, 56
 pork saté with, 28
rainbow vegetables with spicy
  sesame dressing, 127
rice:
 in basic sushi, 48–49
 in hand-rolled sushi with smoked
  salmon, 50
 in lotus chicken packages,
  46–47
 seafood, bundles, 66
rice paper wrappers, 9, 10
 in Vietnamese spring rolls, 38
roll-ups, 5, 23, 55
romaine lettuce, 8, 56

Salads, 53–72
 curried chicken, with grapes, 58
 hot-and-sour slaw with shrimp,
  65
 Indonesian, with coconut-peanut
  dressing, 70
 lemony Thai, packages, 64
 saucy vegetable roll-ups, 72
 seafood rice bundles, 66
 sesame chicken, 60
 soba bundles with chili-garlic
  dressing, 68
 Vietnamese chicken, 57
 Vietnamese fresh mint, 62
salmon:
 grilled miso, with sweet-and-sour
  cucumbers, 80
 hand-rolled sushi with smoked,
  50
salsas:
 mango, 146
 pineapple, 144
 spicy, 143
sashimi, 24
satés, 24
 sauce, 148
Sau, C. K., 30

sauces, 1, 141
 for barbecued tofu wraps, 130
 for Cantonese spring rolls, 42–43
 for curried coconut chicken, 90
 for flaky curry turnovers, 34–36
 for flash-cooked chicken with
  leeks, 87
 for fresh Chinese spring rolls, 40
 gado gado, 55, 70
 ginger teriyaki, 82
 for grilled tempeh with basil, 134
 hot and sour, 88
 for lemongrass beef wraps, 96
 for lemony Thai salad packages,
  64
 for lotus chicken packages, 46–47
 for Malaysian pork rolls, 93
 for mu shu shrimp, 84–86
 peanut, 147
 for pork saté with radicchio, 28
 saté, 148
 for saucy Korean rolls, 92
 for seared garlic beef with
  roasted rainbow peppers, 98
 for Singapore noodles in lettuce
  leaves, 136
 spicy, for saucy vegetable roll-ups,
  72
 spicy sesame for Sichuan-style
  wontons, 30
 sweet and sour, 26
 for tofu sambals, 132
 see also dipping sauces; salsas
saucy vegetable roll-ups, 72
Savoy cabbage, 56
scallops:
 hot-and-sour, with broccoli, 88
 in seafood rice bundles, 66
Schlesinger, Chris, 120
seafood rice bundles, 66
seared:
 garlic beef with roasted rainbow
  peppers, 77, 98

Credits

Many of the dishes featured in the photographs are the work of two talented potters:

Teresa Chang is a second-generation Korean-American whose cross-cultural background has strongly influenced her understated yet elegant porcelain dinnerware and tea accessories. A focus on form, function, and clean structural lines is evidence of her academic training in architecture. Her work is sold internationally. She can be reached directly at (718) 789-9639. Her work is also sold at:

Shi, 233 Elizabeth Street, New York, NY 10012 (212) 334-4330

Global Table, 107 Sullivan Street, New York, NY 10012 (212) 431-5639

Steven Murphy is an American who apprenticed in Japan with Keiichiroh Satoh of Nagano, a master potter. Ash glazes made from wood and leaves give his porcelain bowls, plates, and sake bottles extraordinary and unique finishes. His work reflects the words of his teacher: "You and the clay have to agree on what it will become. Forcing it only makes pottery with no inner beauty." Steven Murphy can be reached at his studio in Boston at (617) 482-5171. His work is also available at:

The Artful Hand, 36 Copley Place, 100 Huntington Avenue, Boston, MA 02116 (617) 262-9601

All remaining props are from:

Felissimo, 10 West 56 Street, New York, NY 10019 (800) 565-6785